"For those struggling with difficult questions about God, faith and life overall, Michael Hidalgo offers insights from Scripture, reflections from his own journey and a healthy dose of humor to guide us all toward a more robust faith in Jesus."

Brad Lomenick, author of *The Catalyst Leader,* former president of Catalyst

"Poet Robert Frost warned about a surplus of 'malevolent guides' in life who 'only have at heart your getting lost.' Michael Hidalgo is a guide on the journey of life you can trust, who only has at heart your finding your way and helping you through life's fogs, furies and failures. This guidebook is a GPS (God Positioning System) for the soul."

Leonard Sweet, author and professor

"Michael Hidalgo does it again! He captures the heart, the hopes, the struggles and the dreams of our generation that nudge us forward toward God. Along the way, he pries our fingers free of shallow thinking and inflexible belief so that we may lay hold of faith more wholly and freely. Hidalgo is a voice you can't afford to miss."

Margaret Feinberg, author of *Fight Back With Joy* and *Wonderstruck*

"If you inherited a rigid, confining faith that doesn't leave you room to breathe, Michael Hildalgo's new book will help you. With wisdom, clarity and a down-to-earth, enjoyable writing style, *Changing Faith* shows how true faith stretches and grows with us, helping us discover God in bigger and deeper ways through life's unexpected and challenging experiences."

Brian D. McLaren, author of *Naked Spirituality*

"Michael has such a genuine heart to see the power of Jesus making a difference in the lives of people. This book is a call to maturity in how we follow Jesus in our modern world that cuts through superficial stock answers and replaces them with real wisdom. There are no pat answers or worn clichés here. Just real stories, honest truths and a better picture of what following Jesus in the twenty-first century can be."

Carl Medearis, author of *Adventures in Saying Yes*

"As our world changes with unprecedented velocity, Michael Hidalgo reminds us that the only constants are God and change itself. He does this by challenging us to consider that our own lens on the world is but one perspective, and invites us to new ways of seeing reality while engaging God and others. Ultimately, this important book helps us understand that faith in flux can lead to a more 'other-centered' life."

Michael John Cusick, author of *Surfing for God,* president, Restoring the Soul

CHANGING FAITH

Questions, Doubts & Choices
About an UNCHANGING GOD

MICHAEL HIDALGO
Foreword by HUGH HALTER

IVP Books
An imprint of InterVarsity Press
Downers Grove, Illinois

InterVarsity Press
P.O. Box 1400, Downers Grove, IL 60515-1426
ivpress.com
email@ivpress.com

InterVarsity Press® is the book-publishing division of InterVarsity Christian Fellowship/USA®, a movement of students and faculty active on campus at hundreds of universities, colleges and schools of nursing in the United States of America, and a member movement of the International Fellowship of Evangelical Students. For information about local and regional activities, visit intervarsity.org.

All Scripture quotations, unless otherwise indicated, are taken from THE HOLY BIBLE, NEW INTERNATIONAL VERSION®, NIV® Copyright © 1973, 1978, 1984, 2011 by Biblica, Inc.™ Used by permission. All rights reserved worldwide.

While any stories in this book are true, some names and identifying information may have been changed to protect the privacy of individuals.

Cover design: Cindy Kiple
Interior design: Beth McGill
Images: calendar: © grgroup/Fotolia.com

ISBN 978-0-8308-3695-6 (print)
ISBN 978-0-8308-9767-4 (digital)

Printed in the United States of America ∞

Library of Congress Cataloging-in-Publication Data
Hidalgo, Michael.
  Changing faith : questions, doubts and choices about an unchanging
God / Michael Hidalgo.
    pages cm
  Includes bibliographical references.
  ISBN 978-0-8308-3695-6 (pbk. : alk. paper)—ISBN 978-0-8308-9767-4 (digital)
  1. God (Christianity)—Immutability. 2. Change—Religious
aspects--Christianity. I. Title.
  BT153.I47.H53 2015
  231—dc23
                                                    2015006638

P	21	20	19	18	17	16	15	14	13	12	11	10	9	8	7	6	5	4	3	2	1
Y	32	31	30	29	28	27	26	25	24	23	22	21	20	19	18	17	16	15			

For my father, Carlos Hidalgo.

We are beauty from ashes.

Contents

Foreword

■■■

Here is a truism. The most important things about any person's life—what you will do, what you will become, and what you will endure and accomplish—are largely based upon one thing: what you believe God to be. No, it's not based on what you believe about the Bible, or what you believe about church, or what you believe about religion or even Christianity. It's simply and irrevocably what and who you believe God to be.

I travel almost every week, mostly speaking and working with Christian leaders and Jesus followers, and I'm becoming more convinced than ever that belief systems do very little for people. The greatest example is Christianity. As the church declines (actually crashes and burns) in Western society, I find a deep, unquenched thirst, even an angst that has millions of Jesus-oriented people straddling a cynicism that will either paralyze and pull them out of organized faith, or push them toward a new, useless fundamentalism.

Is there any other option? Is there any other way we can base our lives upon Jesus without getting high-centered on all the other junk?

I believe there is, and Michael proves it in *Changing Faith*.

I've known Michael for many years. Our churches have shared space. We have both been called to see Jesus come alive in the city of Denver. However, among all the leaders I've run into, Michael has a unique gift of cutting through the red tape of religious confusion and guiding the spiritually open toward holy yet practical ground.

Michael will change your heart on many issues, and even change your mind. You'll be glad he did. And in the end, you'll have a changing faith, one that will bring you to life and make sense to others around you.

Hugh Halter

Introduction

Going Through Changes

■■■

Jesus is the same yesterday, today and tomorrow. However, yesterday, today and tomorrow are not the same at all. A friend of mine told me recently, "There are so many things I am not comfortable with claiming as 100 percent true, but I cannot say they are 100 percent false either." It hasn't always been this way for him.

Most of his life he believed he had the answers to all of life's difficult questions; he was able to vanquish the most brilliant skeptic in a theological argument; and he had a number of degrees from well-respected seminaries around the world.

He continued, "I do not know what is ahead, but I do know I cannot and will not go back to the faith I have clung to for decades. I am done with it." This was not his declaration of renouncing faith, but a recognition that his faith had to change. He was going through a change of faith.

I've had many similar conversations with people over the years. I've been with people who struggle

Jesus is the same yesterday, today and tomorrow. However, yesterday, today and tomorrow are not the same at all.

with doubt, ask questions with no good answers, acknowledge fear, recognize how little we know, grapple with their lack of certainty in God, and talk of their suspicions about the church. Their feelings are rooted in important and difficult questions. Questions such as: How much can we actually know about God and our world? Who is right and who is wrong, and who gets to determine that? Are right and wrong the best categories for our world anymore? Whose "truth" is really true, and is there only one? Do I need God to live a life that matters?

Mind you, these conversations are not with people who have rejected faith in God, the church, religion or spirituality. Rather, these conversations are with faithful men and women exploring a new kind of thinking in the midst of our rapidly changing world.

And our world is changing. Change is the process of moving from somewhere to somewhere else.

From science to business to politics to religion, our world is different every day. We live in a time of new questions, new realities, new technology and new insights that demand new answers. Our world is changing, and that changes everything, including us. It changes the way we live, communicate, think and even the way we believe. This change is sweeping and demands we rethink everything—even our faith.

Like my friend, many of us held to certain beliefs about God, life, faith, church, religion and spirituality as though our lives and faith depended on it, but we cannot hold on to those anymore. We've let go of them, knowing we won't pick them up again.

What's more pressing, however, is the question, What beliefs will we pick up? We know we are moving from somewhere, but we don't exactly know what we are moving toward. Right now, the best we can do is consider what our next best steps should be, rather than deciding what our final destination will be.

And that's what this book is about.

It's not the final word on change, nor is it a deep exploration regarding all the ways our world is changing. My suspicion is that we have accepted that our world is changing, and in the midst of this it would do us well to have some direction. As we struggle for greater understanding, we will explore our faith in the midst of this dynamic, changing world that demands we think in new, fresh and creative ways about God, life, church, religion and spirituality. Which means we have some choices to make, because in the face of change we do not have a choice about making a choice.

We can choose to ignore our changing world. Rather than move from somewhere toward somewhere else, we can hold to the notion that we have all the answers we need, and believe that the final word on God, life and faith has been spoken. We can work to keep things the way they have always been and defend our territory. We can simply refuse to move anywhere and do all we can to stay right here.

Or we can choose cynicism. We can criticize the systems, institutions and those within them who think they have finally arrived. Rather than work creatively and constructively, we can tear down, mock and complain. We can work to destroy where we have been, leaving behind a mound of rubble and ruin for someone else to clean up. In the end we still will not have moved to somewhere.

Or we can choose to give up on the whole enterprise of God and faith altogether, and remain indifferent. We can reject all ideas from yesterday—even the notion that there is a God, let alone one who never changes. We can walk away from religion and spirituality, believing they are tools for a more primitive world. We can abandon where we have been, and not move in any real direction at all.

Or we can come together and develop new ways of thinking, living and engaging God. We can celebrate the place we are moving from. We can accept and embrace the change that is happening all around us. Together we can experience a change of faith. And we can do this with a humble confidence—because while our world is changing, there is a God who is unchanging.

The writer of Hebrews observed, "Jesus Christ is the same yesterday and today and forever" (Hebrews 13:8). God himself spoke through the prophet Malachi saying, "I the LORD do not change" (Malachi 3:6).

To speak of the unchanging God means that God's love, compassion, mercy, faithfulness, grace, love and redemption never change. No matter how much or how fast our world changes, we can always count on his love for us and this world of ours. And his love gives us tremendous freedom.

God needs nothing more; nothing can be added or subtracted. But the same cannot be said of us. How we understand God and speak about him must always grow and expand. And as we grow we are forced to explore, question, consider and reconsider many aspects of our faith. While God might be the same yesterday, today and tomorrow—yesterday, today and tomorrow are not the same at all, and this is the challenge.

Remember, change is the only constant. And time and again God has been faithful to meet people where they are, which means we do not need to be threatened by change. In fact, God is our center in the midst of constant change.

God is on the move, and that has never changed. He invites us to move from somewhere to somewhere else and to trust him in the process. Trusting him is the challenge and the real choice we have to make. Will we trust the unchanging God in our ever-changing world? He invites us to move, which should give us great faith in change. Because, in the end, it's not only about what we do but also what God is doing.

As we grow we are free to count

> **God is our center in the midst of constant change.**

on God's love, care, concern and activity in this world. Because of that we are able to confidently explore new, different and better ways to think and speak about him.

This is the invitation I wish to extend—that we would be open to our beliefs growing and expanding as we walk alongside one another from somewhere to somewhere else and explore our belief in our unchanging God in the midst of our changing world.

In the back of the book is a discussion guide to help us as we consider moving from somewhere toward somewhere. This guide is designed for groups, since we were not meant to travel alone. You can use the discussion guide with a friend, your book club, small group or family. My hope is it will help us to be honest about where we are in the midst of our changing faith as we wrestle with our questions, doubts and choices about the unchanging God.

1

From Closed to Open

∎∎∎

few weeks before I started middle school, I discovered the opinions and beliefs I had been taught my entire life were not the only way of seeing our world. My parents left the life they built in New York and moved across the country to a town I had never heard of: Grand Rapids, Michigan. The day my father told our family about moving to Michigan, he called it the Midwest. I was mortified.

How could we survive amid farmers, tractors, cornfields, cows and kids in tattered overalls? In the months leading up to our move, I was heartsick. To my delight, when we finally moved, I discovered it wasn't all farmers, tractors, cornfields and cows, and no one wore tattered overalls. It seemed normal enough—until the first day of school.

My new school began each year with an all-student assembly in the gymnasium. The first day came and I was a nervous wreck. I wore my coolest outfit in a meager attempt to impress my new classmates, which did little to cover my looming insecurity about going to a new school. I arrived at the school building, had trouble finding my locker, got a little turned around and ended up being a few minutes late for the assembly.

I told myself it would be fine. Surely, no one would notice one student slipping in the back of the packed gym a few minutes late.

I finally made my way to the gymnasium, cracked open the back door and slipped through quietly. I looked up and to my absolute dismay every single student was staring at me. What I thought was the back door was actually a door directly behind the stage and opposite the bleachers filled with students.

In less than five seconds I went from the "new kid" to the "kid who interrupted the school assembly." Our principal, who stood on the stage, stopped, turned and looked at me with a confused expression. I did my best to play it cool. So I smiled at the principal and gave him a quick, confident head nod.

Each step I took sounded like a clap of thunder on the hardwood floor in the gym, now dead silent as hundreds of students watched me walk toward the bleachers. As I rounded the stage, the front row of the bleachers seemed like it was hundreds of feet away. Just before I sat down I offered up an awkward wave to my fellow students.

It was a brutal introduction to middle school. I sensed this was the low point in my thirteen years of life. It could not get any worse. My face was red hot, and my heart smashed against my ribs. The silence lingered on and was eventually broken by the muffled laughs of students behind me. Then I heard someone say, "What is he wearing?"

I was wrong. It just got worse.

I imagined the person who said this couldn't be serious. This was the best my wardrobe had to offer. I wore an Ocean Pacific sweatshirt with neon-colored surfboards on the front. Beneath the sweatshirt I wore a hot pink polo shirt—with the collar popped. Nicely accenting my bright attire: a pair of gray Bugle Boy pocket pants, with the cuffs pegged. And tying the outfit together nicely was a pair of Reebok high-tops featuring double Velcro closures.

I was confident my outfit would be a smash hit, and thought I would be the envy of every kid in the school. It turns out I was dead wrong. What was cool in New York was not so cool in Michigan. It would have helped to be aware of this fact before the first day of school, when I endured my walk of shame. I quickly learned that as normal as I thought my culture and the lenses through which I saw it were, they were not normal for everyone.

It did not take long to figure out there were many more differences about the culture and lenses of others in this new town, differences that were far more important than what I chose to wear. Over the next several years I learned how blind I was to the lenses I had grown up using. I never even knew they existed until I saw the world through other lenses not my own.

I learned about the different ways people understood family, politics and even God himself. This confused me a great deal, because many of those who saw the world differently were Christians, but not like the Christians I knew in New York.

The more I learned, the more doubt crept into my life. If these people believed in the same God as the people in New York, then why were there so many lenses? How could it be that Christians could believe so many different things about God, life, faith, church, religion and spirituality? After a while, I grew tired of hearing various opinions, debates and arguments.

I came to see the one thing that didn't change was how many Christians believed their lenses were the *only* lenses worth looking through, and I wondered why people were unwilling to look through the lenses of others. Many of us refuse to consider other viewpoints. Perhaps it will challenge our understanding of the world. Even

> I came to see how many Christians believed their lenses were the *only* lenses worth looking through.

worse, it may reveal to us where we are wrong or misguided.

As we confront the realities of our changing faith, we have to wrestle with whether we are willing to look through others' lenses or only look through our own. Are we willing to move from one set of lenses toward multiple lenses? Will we be open to new ways of seeing, knowing and thinking, or will we remain closed?

NEW LENSES

A few weeks ago my wife and I met a couple named Drew and Trisha. We ended up conversing with them for more than an hour. Drew grew up in a devout Catholic family. He was baptized as an infant, went through confirmation and participated in the tradition of First Communion. It was all he ever knew and believed.

He held deeply to his faith during college and was like a Catholic missionary, telling anyone who would listen about what he believed and why they should believe it too. As zealous as he was for his faith, he finally encountered people who saw the world through different lenses, and it changed everything.

After college Drew got a job requiring extensive travel. In his travels he met Buddhists, atheists, Hindus, Mormons, Muslims and Jews. He discovered all sorts of people who were good, kind and loving, and many who loved Jesus but were not Catholic. He had trouble understanding these experiences because he had been told his entire life "those people" were nothing like him. "They were better people than a lot of Catholics I knew," he told us. He continued, "There was a whole other world of life and faith out there that caused me to question mine."

Drew saw there are millions of lenses in our world, which caused him to see how limited his lenses were. This led to his love-hate relationship with religion, which, to this day, is mostly hate. He abandoned all organized religion and claims to be a "spiritual wanderer." Still, he cannot let go of the idea of God. He said, "I believe in a Supreme Being. I just don't think he entangles himself in all the religious stuff we get into."

Drew's wife listened patiently, and when he paused for a moment she said, "Then he married a Lutheran!" Trisha grew up in a small town in Minnesota "where everyone was Lutheran." After attending college for two years, she became a professional athlete. Like Drew, she met people from all walks of life with many different lenses. She too is indifferent to religion, but more interested than her husband.

They have considered being a part of a faith community, but finding connection to God has been difficult. Their story is the same for many of us who, like Drew and Trisha, grew up in the Christian faith only to abandon it years later. When we are exposed to new lenses, it's natural to assume our old lenses are bad or wrong. Many conclude we need to throw out the old lenses altogether.

This can happen because many of us were given a faith tradition of doctrine bounded by narrow thinking, and we believe this faith never changes. We grew up being told our way of thinking and living is the one right way. Because of this, when we discover something outside of our faith that appears to be true, we have to make a hard choice: this *or* that. It cannot be both. We either jettison the lenses we were given at an early age or push away the new lenses.

If we jettison the old, our lenses may change but the way we use them hasn't. We merely exchange one set for another, while remaining closed to interpreting the world with a broader viewpoint. We remain content to see the world through one set. When we do this, we are closed.

Some of us encounter other ways of seeing our world, but rather than throwing out the old lenses, we push away the new and root ourselves more firmly in our original way of seeing things. In doing so we dismiss other ways of seeing the world and label them as wrong. Instead of looking through multiple lenses, we go so far as to refine the one set of lenses we have.

The more refined the lenses, the more defensive we become. We tell ourselves we must protect our sliver of truth from outside intrusions. Over time, we no longer see things as they are, but judge everything as good or bad. The more we judge, the more refined our lenses become.

In this place we often operate out of fear and self-interest, not out of love and concern for others. We surround ourselves with others who share our view of the world—those who think, live, act and look like us. Together, we convince ourselves we are right. It's easy to do. After all, if everyone we associate with thinks this way, then it can't be wrong. This accepted, collective thinking only cements us in our way of seeing the world.

In the times when I do this, I end up defining myself by what I am not. And there is nothing less compelling than people who define themselves by what they are not. My friend Paul discovered this when he started a church more than ten years ago.

> There is nothing less compelling than people who define themselves by what they are not.

Not long after he started his church it thrived and experienced rapid growth. However, it didn't last long. Within three years of starting his church, people who had been there from the beginning began leaving. He couldn't figure out why until he asked someone why she left. She said, "You and this church do things the way you do because you want to be different from other churches. *Everything is about what you are not.*"

That statement woke him up to his narrow lenses. For the first time he saw their vision of the church came out of what they were against, and they were great at being against a lot of things. He told me he made the mistake of believing that saying what he was against was a good way of saying what he was for. He was so dialed in to what he was against, he never created a new, better path forward. He ended up becoming stale, boring and horribly uncreative. For those who were a part of his church, being against everything got old quick, and they moved on.

Paul and the leadership in his church were closed. They believed they had the lenses they needed, and they protected those at all costs. They moved backward, which is not the way to move forward. We cannot dig our heels in and tell ourselves we need to go back to the way things were.

Doing this is ignoring the wise words of the Teacher in Ecclesiastes. He instructed, "Do not say, 'Why were the old days better than these?' For it is not wise to ask such questions" (Ecclesiastes 7:10). To move backward is to admit defeat. It's like playing a game not to lose.

What we forget is we have already won. We have nothing to fear. On the cross Jesus "disarmed the powers and authorities, . . . triumphing over them" (Colossians 2:15). We live in a world that belongs to God, who said, "the world is mine, and all that is in it" (Psalm 50:12). With a viewpoint like this, we don't have to be closed. We can be open.

This is not easy; sometimes we have to be forced open. There will be people who challenge, disturb and push us. However, when we are open we learn more about ourselves, others and the God of the universe.

EVERYTHING YOU KNOW IS (NOT) WRONG

My friend Ryan grew up on a farm in rural Indiana. The world he grew up in was the same picture of the Midwest that caused me such consternation. In his senior class there were no African Americans, no one was openly gay and no one affiliated with any religion but Christianity. His life in Indiana was comfortable. Ryan was surrounded by people just like him.

In his world, different ideas about religion, sexual orientation and even politics were distant realities he heard about only on television. He saw the world through the lenses of Christian Middle America. Here he sensed an invitation to follow God into ministry, which initially meant becoming a pastor in a local church.

He moved to Denver to go to seminary. Not too long after he started classes, his years of faithful church attendance, participation in the church and reading the Bible felt dull. On top of this, he met many who viewed the world through different lenses.

Many of his coworkers had no affiliation with any particular faith group. They believed Christians were irrelevant, judgmental and shaming. After many conversations with them, Ryan had questions about his faith, which led him to move out of his comfort zone. He wasn't sure what he would find, but he knew the lenses he had grown up with were not the only ones worth looking through. Ryan saw his was a changing faith.

In his desire to expand his viewpoint on the world, Ryan found himself in places he had never been, surrounded by people who were nothing like him. He started spending one night each week working with the chronically homeless in Denver. He had no idea what lay ahead, but this experience pulled him down a rabbit hole that in some ways shattered his original lenses and in other ways expanded them.

Ryan met men and women from different cultures, became friends with those of different religions and spent time with people of different sexual orientation. He discovered how tightly he held to stereotypes and assumptions about people. In his connection with others who were not like him, Ryan was continually challenged to confront his anxiety and fear. For the first time he awoke to the depths of God's love and grace among men and women considered by some to be beyond the loving reach of God.

Ryan met God through men and women who live on the ragged edges of society, and this led to a new conversion. Ryan's viewpoint was not just born again once but again and again and again. This renewed way of seeing things broadened his understanding of how "wide and long and high and deep" the love of God is (Ephesians 3:18).

But there was something Ryan did not do. Rather than throw away the lenses he was given in Indiana, he held on to them. This set of lenses, when added to the new sets he found on the streets of Denver, allowed him to see the world more broadly than ever before. Ryan has eyes to see the love, grace and mercy of God in ways few can, whether that be on a rural farm in Indiana or in an alley in urban Denver. He moved from one set of lenses to multiple sets, and in the process he didn't throw out his old lenses.

Experiences like Ryan's are a gift. They allow us to see the world through new lenses. When we come together with others who do not think, look, talk or believe like us, and sit, listen, and share, we have an opportunity to see the heart of God in new ways, and allow his grace to continually transform us. In those moments, we are able to see through many lenses.

In doing so, we lose something but gain so much more. Our viewpoint opens wider, we are exposed to blind spots and are better able to see God at work in this broad, divergent, ever-changing world. And this is good thing.

If the only way of understanding and encountering God were the way I presently understand him, it would be a dry, boring, predictable and stale world. We must remain open so we can fully engage the heart of God and embrace this world as he does. When we do this we can see with his eyes, hear with his ears and speak with his voice. We can live with a vibrant, dynamic, changing faith.

It's easy to spot people whose lives are open. They are neither cynical about our world nor critical of others. In their depth and ma-

> We must remain open so we can fully engage the heart of God and embrace this world as he does.

turity they are not easily offended. If anything, they seem insatiably curious. When it comes to others and our world, their first step is observation, not judgment. They are honest with themselves, and when they speak, everyone seems to listen. They are willing to be out front, to take risks and to be called heretics because deep inside they know their way of seeing the infinite, unchanging God is finite and changing.

Chances are many of us are somewhere between open and closed. We are open to some things and closed to others. Whatever is the truth about ourselves, we should know this: God is at work and does not wait for us to respond positively or negatively.

This does not mean we completely abandon everything we have ever known. We must discern what we should hold on to from yesterday, what we need to throw away today and what new things we ought to pick up as we head toward tomorrow. Faithful men and women have always done this.

They had the eyes to see there was always more than one way of understanding, seeing and knowing God. They were open. As times changed, the way they understood God changed too. This is normal. Any time a new way of thinking emerges, there are new realities to wrestle through, new things to consider, and old boundaries that need to be erased.

2

From Certainty to Probability

■■■

We live each day walking on a thin veneer of certainty regarding what may happen to us. We fail to see that the best we can do is to live with a sense of probability about what might happen. Most of the time this veneer works well, but then something upsets our normal routine. I learned this just before my daughter was born.

One morning my wife and I saw her doctor for a routine checkup. Her doctor is a fun-loving person who always entered the room with a smile. Never hurried, she took time to catch up with us, ask how we were doing, and often spoke about her children. But this time was different.

She entered the room, stared at my wife's chart and barely acknowledged we were in the room. After flipping through the chart for more than a minute, she set it down, looked at both of us and said in a completely calm voice, "You need to have an ultrasound."

When people in the medical community get calm, I get nervous. I call it the "medical calm." My wife is a nurse, and we have friends who are doctors, so I know what it means when they get calm. It means something is serious, and they need to think and speak clearly. She explained my wife had lost weight, and since she was late into the pregnancy, it was cause for concern.

We walked down the hall into another exam room where a woman performed the ultrasound. She was so focused she barely said a word to either of us, which made me more nervous. After the ultrasound, my wife's doctor came back to explain our daughter had lost weight in the womb, the umbilical cord and placenta were dying, and the best thing to do was induce labor.

Before we left for the hospital she explained there could be physical and developmental delays, and once we arrived at the hospital, another doctor who specialized in high-risk births would come and see us. My head was spinning and I was sick to my stomach as I heard our doctor use words like "high risk" and "serious issues" about our daughter.

What followed was the longest twelve hours of my life. During that time we learned our daughter lost nearly a pound. She was not getting the proper nutrition she needed, which affected her growth and would likely cause lifelong setbacks. Family and friends stopped by and prayed over my wife and our daughter. Many more called us from around the country to tell us they too were praying. All day long I sat with my wife completely powerless. We had zero control.

There was nothing we could do to change the situation. We were brought face-to-face with the fact we did not control anything. Finally, at 11:25 p.m. my daughter was born. The first thing the doctor said was, "She looks healthy!" She was quite surprised. They immediately examined her, and found she was heavier than they expected. They compared the ultrasound from the morning to our daughter and were puzzled.

Somehow, the weight she lost in the womb had all come back. When I finally held her for the first time, I wept, knowing I was in the midst of the miraculous. To be clear, I shed a lot of tears at the birth of my other two children too. But these were tears of relief, unspeakable joy and endless gratitude. Every bit of anxiety we had left the room. I held a miracle in my arms—and I didn't do anything.

This is hard for me to admit, because I like to control things. I'm not sure I would say I am a controlling person, but I do like to believe I can handle anything that comes my way. Even in difficult situations I like to think I can fix whatever the problem is. But then there are times when I am confronted with how limited my ability to control my life really is.

That day in the hospital, any semblance of control was ripped out of my hands, and it was painful. Nothing prepared my wife and me for what happened. All our plans went out the window.

The truth is, my everyday life is the same as the day my daughter was born. I am no more in control today than I was on that day more than ten years ago. This is my constant struggle. Still I want to think I am in control and I have all my bases covered. But I don't and never will. Even self-control comes only by the Spirit (see Galatians 5:22-23).

We often live with a desire to control things because it gives us security and certainty. We want control so badly we even try to control God. We like to think we can control how and where and when he will act. It's almost as if we place boundaries around him, box him in and create a framework for him. We look for him in all the expected places, thinking he will work within the small world we create for him. But God is not confined by our small plans, and he works in ways far outside our supposed span of control.

Just when I am tempted to think I've got my God boundaries nicely drawn, he comes around and blows my way of thinking sky high. Placing boundaries around God is nothing new. Humans have done it for thousands of years. In the primitive world these boundaries were literal borders that divided nations and states.

TAKING DIRT

Naaman was a valiant soldier from a place called Aram in Syria, where the god Rimmon was served. Naaman discovered he had leprosy and was desperate for healing. At that time, a diagnosis of leprosy was a death sentence. It was a contagious disease, and those with it were quarantined, forced to live outside the city. Lepers were cut off from family, friends, work and everything else. It is no surprise Naaman was desperate.

In his search for healing, he learned about a man in Israel who could heal him. Naaman traveled across the border to find this man so he could be healed. Of course, this meant placing faith in another god to heal him, because the god Rimmon was not from the Israel. He found Elisha the prophet. When Naaman arrived at Elisha's house, Elisha sent word to Naaman to dip himself in the Jordan River seven times. Naaman did just that and found his leprosy was totally gone. The God of Israel healed him.

Naaman went back to Elisha and said, "Please let me, your servant, be given as much earth as a pair of mules can carry, for your servant will never again make burnt offerings and sacrifices to any other god but the LORD" (2 Kings 5:17).

An odd request, no? Of all the things he could have asked for, Naaman asked to take dirt home. But it makes total sense when we understand the way Naaman thought of the world. In his day people believed gods were regional. Each nation had their own gods and believed their gods were local. While the gods had power, they were limited by zip code.

This meant the God who healed him had undeniable power, but, as Naaman believed, only within the borders of Israel. So, if Naaman brought some of Israel home with him, then he could offer sacrifices to the Lord in Aram. It was simple logic. Earth from Israel would allow God to hear Naaman's prayers.

Naaman failed to see that God doesn't do boundaries—not then, not now. Today, we create boundaries around denominations, political parties, nations and theologies. But God doesn't play by these rules and cannot be contained by the boxes we put him in. God is not just outside the box, he blew the box up. Too often we attempt to redraw the boundaries God blurs or put the box he has blown up back together. We fail to see many of the lines we draw do not come from God at all.

Last week a friend told me of a conversation he had with a person who said, "I cannot understand how someone could be a Christian and a Republican." Then, the very next day he had another conversation with someone who said, "How can anyone be a Democrat and call themselves a Christian?" This really happened.

There are, no doubt, all kinds of reasons these people would say such things. But both of them are guilty of the same thing. They have imported God into their framework and believe he will operate only within their preconceived notions of what is right and good. More than that, both seem to forget that God not only is not a Republican or a Democrat—God is not American.

We so often live as though our way of thinking and of doing things is also God's way. We divide over issues, use the Bible to defend our position and claim we are on God's side. But whenever we reduce the big, massive, expansive, unchanging God to our way of doing things, we are attempting to create God in our image. And this does not stop at politics.

Many can admit God is not a Republican or Democrat, but we must also admit he is not Baptist, Episcopalian, Catholic, Lutheran, Reformed, Methodist, Presbyterian, nondenominational or any of the more than forty thousand denominations in the world. Whenever we attempt to make God more like us, there is a good

> **Whenever we attempt to make God more like us, there is a good chance we become less like him.**

chance we become less like him. We must remember God does not observe all the dividing lines we have set up.

God is not interested in religious divisions. Rather, he has destroyed the barriers and "the dividing wall of hostility" keeping us apart. He calls all of us into the place of existing as "one new humanity" (Ephesians 2:14-16). This is what Jesus constantly taught and revealed. This is most apparent in what was central to the life and ministry of Jesus: meals.

HOW BIG IS GOD'S TABLE?

We have, in large part today, lost what it means to have meals together. "I'm concerned that Americans are losing that place of meeting," Maya Angelou said. "There are very few times we can be more intimate as to share food together." She went on to recount how we eat our food in a rush before we are on to the next thing. Today, we may have a few meals around the holidays that bring us together. But this was not the case with Jesus.

The Gospels tell us Jesus went from house to house eating and dining with people. He ate with his disciples, with immigrants, with the religious, with sinners, with the rich and with the poor. Many of Jesus' teachings and parables occurred while he was sitting at a dinner table.

While eating a meal with the religious, he once told a parable about a man who prepared a massive feast and invited the regularly expected guests. But none of them came because they were too busy with life and business. So the host of the feast told his servant to go into the streets, the alleys, the roadways and under the bridges and bring in the "the poor, the crippled, the blind and the lame" (Luke 14:21-24).

The people listening to Jesus did not miss the point. Those who assumed they were in and expected an invitation to the banquet were out. And those who believed there was no way they would ever receive an invitation to the banquet were in. When it comes to the table of Jesus, there are no boundaries, because it is not about people trying to get in at all. Jesus taught that God invites any who will come to sit and feast with him. And Jesus did this all the time.

Jesus ate with tax collectors who were known for corruption and exploitation of the poor, and he ate with the poor who were exploited by the tax collectors. Jesus sat at the table with the hardcore religious, and he ate dinner with the sinners the religious despised. He pushed against every social, religious and political barrier set up in his day and ate with all who welcomed him to their table. His practice of meals teaches us the only boundaries that exist with regard to the love of God are ones we create.

> The only boundaries that exist with regard to the love of God are ones we create.

God destroys our barriers and erases our boundaries, so we may want to practice the art of letting go of ours. Maybe then we'd have a better chance of seeing all the miraculous ways he works in our ever-changing world, and then we could join him in what he is already doing. As we live out our changing faith, we need to move from seeing God as predictable and move toward seeing him as unpredictable.

AN UNPREDICTABLE GOD

Science confirms we live in an unpredictable world. For centuries modern minds thought they understood the way the universe worked. Given enough numbers, equations, formulas, data, research and experiments, they could explain everything. The brightest minds in the world organized the laws of our universe into a discipline now called classical mechanics. For a time, they were confident in their ability to explain unbelievably complex realities. They did this because they were rooted in certainty. But this did not last.

A little less than one hundred years ago scientists discovered unexplained phenomenon in our world at the smallest levels of existence. All their laws, experiments and theories could not make

sense of what they saw. They learned our macroworld is quite or-
derly. While at the same time, at the smallest levels of matter, our
world appears chaotic. Physicists have since learned not to ask
questions of certainty; they now ask questions of probability.

As scientists uncovered this new way of understanding the world,
Albert Einstein struggled to come to grips with a world that was not
well-ordered and predictable. In response to emerging theories of
how the world works, Einstein said, "God does not play dice with
the universe." In response to Einstein, friend and colleague Niels
Bohr replied, "Stop telling God what to do." Bohr's words are as
much for us today as they were for Einstein a century ago.

We often prefer to speak on behalf of God in an attempt to explain him with absolute certainty, but we must recognize we will
never be able to fully explain God, the One who is unknowable and
endlessly knowable.

It's no wonder we speak about God being massive and beyond
comprehension. For thousands of years people have spoken about
him being the God of the universe. Even when we take a moment
to contemplate the God who is love, we are confronted with the
reality that he cannot and will not be controlled.

Yet, as big and wild as he is, he is also close to each of us, closer
then our next breath. The writer of Genesis says that God breathed
into the first human the "breath of life" and the man "became a
living being" (Genesis 2:7). The word for "breath" in the Hebrew
language is *ruah*. This word is also used to speak of the Spirit of
God—the one who gives us life.

The incomprehensibly vast God of the universe is the same one
who gives us our breath. God is out there and right here and everywhere in between. Which means he is big enough to defy control,
and yet at the same time is exactly what we need each day of our
life. He's that big and that small. How do we even begin to describe
a God like that?

BEING WHAT WE OBSERVE

One way the biblical writers try to explain God is by describing him as light. The first thing Genesis speaks of in the creation narrative is God bringing forth light. The psalmists say God's light overcomes the darkness in our world. In Revelation, John promises one day the earth will no longer experience night because God will be our light. Jesus declares himself to be the light of the world. The rabbis comment on this, saying light is the splendor of the divine presence.

But does this really clear things up? Light is not like anything else in our world. It is a constant, everyday experience, but at the same time we struggle to explain exactly what it is. As familiar as light is, the most brilliant minds still seem mystified.

In the early eighteenth century Isaac Newton proposed light consisted of particles traveling at great speed. As such, we cannot observe these particles with the naked eye. Newton's theory held strong for nearly one hundred years, until Thomas Young claimed light is not a particle but a wave. Young set up an experiment that proved his theory true, and in doing so turned the scientific world on its head.

Like Newton, Young's theory of light lasted for nearly one hundred years, until observations again suggested light consists of particles. One might think Thomas Young's experiments, which showed light to be a wave, would be proven false. However, when Young's experiment was conducted again, it yielded the same results. It showed light was a wave. So, the conclusion was simple: light is both particles and waves.

If that is not confusing enough, scientists discovered light shows itself to be waves or particles based on how it is observed. Which means if a person is looking for light to show itself as waves, it will show itself as waves, and the same is true of particles. Light appears to behave differently depending on how a person seeks to observe it.

Keep in mind, what scientists observed was light—that never changed. What changed was their interaction with it, and that somehow caused light to reveal itself differently. Light, which is so common, is difficult to wrap our minds around. Isn't this like God?

No wonder the biblical writers describe God as light. He never changes but is faithful to respond to us and be exactly what we need him to be. My friend Tomas knows all about this.

Tomas grew up on the eastern side of Cuba. His mother had a glimmer of understanding of God from her childhood. Other than that, as a boy he knew nothing about God or a supreme being of any kind. He and his family were well-acquainted with struggle and oppression. One evening the years of frustration brought his mother to the brink, and she planned to take her own life.

Tomas found her with a knife; she held it to her chest and warned him not to come any closer. Something came over him and he felt like someone walked into the room and stood right next to him. For the first time in his life he called out to something or someone. He fell to his knees, and then his mother released the knife. But the knife did not fall on the ground. It floated gently to a table in the room and touched down softly as though someone laid it there. He and his mother were unable to speak or move.

Tomas needed God that desperate night in Cuba, and God showed himself to be exactly what he needed. That night his mother and he gave their whole selves to whoever was in that room, even though they couldn't explain it and did not know who it was. Tomas is not alone.

There are millions of stories just like his. Addicts who find God in the throes of addiction. Parents who find God in the birth of a child. Adventurers who find God in the beauty of a mountain peak. Activists who find God in the face of the poor. The God who is too big to be controlled is the very one in our midst. He is not far from any of us, and if we reach out for him we will find him. He shows up within our borders, but also far outside of anything we can create or even imagine. We must not forget God is not so much in a world of our making, but we are in his. There is tremendous hope in this because God shows himself everywhere. He even crosses the boundaries we create and invites us to see how he works outside them.

THE WIND BLOWS WHEREVER IT PLEASES

The church has struggled with this since its beginning. In the book of Acts the story of how God moves begins predictably enough. Those who followed Jesus and believed in him received the Holy Spirit in Jerusalem during the feast of Pentecost. This was just the beginning. God's Spirit was on the move.

We should not be surprised by this. Jesus said, "The wind blows wherever it pleases. You hear its sound, but you cannot tell where it comes from or where it is going. So it is with everyone born of the Spirit" (John 3:8). Even so, some had a tough time imagining how far God would go in reaching all people.

Luke told a story about the apostle Peter's surprise by the movement of God. One afternoon Peter had a vision from God. He saw a sheet come down from heaven filled with all kinds of animals, and a voice said, "'Get up, Peter. Kill and eat.' 'Surely not, Lord!' Peter replied. 'I have never eaten anything impure or unclean'" (Acts 10:13-14). According to Peter's religious tradition he was not supposed to eat certain animals. How could God ask him to do something that betrayed his faith and clearly violated Scripture?

After Peter had the vision, some people from the household of Cornelius, a Roman centurion, visited Peter. They invited him to go with them to teach Cornelius and his family about Jesus.

It was against the law for a Jewish man like Peter to associate with or visit people like Cornelius. How could God want Peter to be around people like this? However, as Peter learned, God is not concerned about our boundaries and laws.

When Peter entered Cornelius's house he remembered the vision and said, "God does not show favoritism" (Acts 10:34). While Peter spoke to them, those present received the Holy Spirit, just as Jesus' followers in Jerusalem had.

When Peter returned to Jerusalem, some of the religious criticized Peter for going to the home of a Roman soldier and having a meal there. Peter responded by telling them the story about the vision, the invitation, how he saw God move and how those in Cornelius's household received the Holy Spirit too. He then said to his critics, "Who was I to think that I could stand in God's way?" (Acts 11:17).

We all should ask Peter's question: Who are we to stand in God's way? Who are we to draw lines, craft barriers, construct boxes, create in-groups and out-groups, and determine the ways and places God will work?

When Peter's critics heard his story, they celebrated. They experienced a change of faith and saw God does not play by our rules or see the world from our limited viewpoint. He cannot be controlled any more than we can control the wind.

> God does not play by our rules or see the world from our limited viewpoint.

This is good news. He is the God who is nearer to us than our next breath, as distant as the furthest galaxies in our universe and everywhere in between. Our joy is found in moving from seeing God as limited to our small world to discovering that he is unpredictable. God is beyond control and is moving in places we never thought possible.

How do we explain that?

3

From Definition to Description

■■■

Thousands of years ago, humans had an overwhelming sense there were forces at work they could not explain. They believed someone or something controlled everything they experienced. Over time myths developed about gods and goddesses. These myths explained the beginning of the world, where humans came from and how the gods came to hold power.

Men and women created images and idols of these gods. Idols symbolized and represented the divine presence on this earth. Every time a temple was built for the worship of a god, it was filled it with images and idols. The Assyrians worshiped Ashur and Shamash, and symbolized the presence of these gods with images engraved on large disks. They referred to these symbols as "the image of the great gods" and believed they represented the gods' presence on earth.

Over time, worshipers treated idols as though they were the gods themselves. What once was only a symbol of the divine became divine itself. A legendary, rabbinic story about Abraham tells how he confronted his father Terah, an idol maker, who forgot these were just carvings of wood and stone. Abraham wanted to wake his father up so he would remember these idols were not the actual presence of living gods.

On one occasion Terah was away and asked Abraham to look after his idol business. During this time a woman came with fine flour to pay for the purchase of an idol. When she left, Abraham took a large stick and smashed all of his father's idols but the largest one. Abraham placed the stick he used to demolish the smaller idols in the hands of the large idol.

When Terah returned and saw the broken idols, he asked Abraham what happened. Abraham explained the idols argued over who would get the fine flour. Then, in a fit of rage, the large idol took the stick and smashed all the smaller idols.

Terah, not believing a word of it, said to his son, "Do I look like an idiot? They are not alive!" To which Abraham replied, "Do you hear what you are saying? And yet you worship them?" (*Genesis Rabbah* 38:13). Terah imagined these idols were the actual embodied presence of the gods on earth.

God understood the human inclination to mistake idols for the gods. This is why he told the people of Israel not to create an idol "in the form of anything in heaven above or on the earth beneath or in the waters below" (Exodus 20:4). God's instruction to his people was his way of telling them he can never be reduced to an idol. No matter what they created, it would never be an accurate reflection of who he was and is. More than this, how exactly would they begin to conceive of an image that represented God?

When God gave the command not to create an idol, the people of Israel had just been freed from slavery in Egypt, where they had been for over four hundred years. They cried out because of the brutality of their slave drivers. God heard their cries and brought them out of the land of slavery. When he led them out of slavery he showed himself during the day as a pillar of cloud and at night a pillar of fire (Exodus 13:22).

He led them to a sea, where the Egyptian army hunted them down. God opened the sea, allowing his people to cross to the other side on dry ground. When the Egyptians entered the same path through the sea, the waters closed in on them and destroyed the Egyptian military. God continued to provide for them, giving Israel bread from heaven, and when they were thirsty, he provided water from a rock.

God invited Israel to be his special people, and spoke to them about what it means to live as his people in this world. He would be their King, and they would be his people. God came to them in an unbelievable display: thunder and lightning, an earthquake, a cloud covering the mountain, and a trumpet so loud the people trembled. Then God spoke to them.

Within a few months of leaving Egypt their encounters with God revealed him as compassionate, a protector, a provider and a king. How do you create an idol representing this God? We learn the answer to that question when Moses left the people to meet with God on the mountain. He was gone so long they feared he was dead. So the people went to Aaron, Moses' brother, and said, "Make us gods" (Exodus 32:1). These are the same words God spoke in Genesis 1 when he said, "Let us make mankind" (Genesis 1:26). This shows us that idolatry reverses the order of creation. When we create idols we step into the place of the Creator and fashion him in our image.

The people collected gold and made an idol in the image of a calf. Aaron said to them, "These are your gods, Israel, who brought you up out of Egypt" (Exodus 32:4). With that, they bowed down and worshiped the idol. Notice they did not say, "This is an image representing your gods who brought you out of Egypt." The people allowed the symbol to become the thing it was supposed to symbolize. For them, the image of the calf was god.

It may seem odd to choose an idol in the image of a calf, but it was what they knew. In Egypt, the god Apis was symbolized as a calf, and he was associated with Egyptian kings. The people had just left Egypt after being there for centuries. They crafted a god—an idol—based on what they knew, which is what we always do.

Today, physical idols are no longer in fashion. We do not melt earrings in the fire to create golden calves. However, we do fashion God into who we think he is. Just as Israel was influenced by the culture and religion of Egypt, all kinds of influences shape how we think of God. But in our culture we have replaced idols with ideas.

ENCOUNTERING THE DIVINE

There is no shortage of ideas about God in our world today. We call these ideas "theology" or "doctrine." Theology is our way of organizing our thoughts, ideas and questions about God. There is nothing wrong with this. We *should* talk about God. In fact, our changing faith demands that we never stop talking about God.

We should speak about how he was understood yesterday, how we experience him today and how we hope he will be understood tomorrow. Theology is an attempt to explain humanity's experience of the divine. Each time we speak about God—how we experience him, how we understand him and what we believe about him—we practice theology.

> Theology is an attempt to explain humanity's experience of the divine.

A few weeks ago my friend Tom told me about his time spent in the Collegiate Peaks Wilderness area in Colorado. This area has eight different peaks soaring at more than 14,000 feet. It is riddled with high alpine lakes, streams and meadows strewn with wildflowers. While there, Tom was in a valley where the leaves of the trees were at peak color, the sun cast its rays through the clouds and rising above all of this was a rugged, snow-covered mountain peak.

His photos made the landscape seem more beautiful than if I had been there myself. One photo was especially stunning. He stared at it in amazement, smiled and said, "This one . . . it is so

God!" I knew exactly what he meant. Being in the midst of God's good, beautiful world led him to an experience with the divine and caused him to worship.

His simple words well expressed the good God who holds all things together, the God who adores this world and all that is in it. He reflected on the God who is creative and delights in the beauty. His one small statement said so much. His words about his experience of and with God in the wilderness were his way of practicing theology.

Tom is not alone. Many of us have moments when we experience God with us, right now. Early this past summer I spent a day of silence and solitude at a retreat center outside Denver. When I woke up I didn't feel like spending a day alone. I had a lot on my mind and heart. I felt restless, agitated and discouraged. The last thing I wanted to do was spend a day in prayer and contemplation.

When I arrived at the retreat center, I could not sit still, so I walked around the property. I told God I needed a light day, and felt like playing and laughing. My heart was heavy with many things, and I needed levity. I walked toward a small grove of trees, saw something move and stopped. Then I saw three deer bedding down under the trees. None of them stood up or ran away. They just stared at me without a hint of fear.

I stood completely still for more than ten minutes, walked closer to them, removed my shoes and sat down less than fifteen feet from them. We sat like this for more than an hour. There I was, sitting under pine trees with three deer. It seemed ridiculous, and I kept laughing to myself as I sat with them. I had a deep sense God gave me the levity I asked for. It was just what I needed. It allowed me to open up and be honest with myself and with God about what was stirring in my heart.

My day, which began with so much inner turmoil, turned out to be one of the best days of the summer. At the end of the day I left the retreat center, and just as I reached my car a deer ran right toward me. It stopped a short distance from me and stared curiously at me. After a few minutes of our stare down, it turned, ran a few steps, stopped and turned back toward me. It did this several times and finally bounded away into the woods. If I were in a C. S. Lewis novel, I would have followed my friend into the woods.

As I drove away, I possessed a keen awareness I was on holy ground. The entire day was a brush with the divine. And when we attempt to describe these experiences with the God of the universe, we practice theology, which is unbelievably important. We must take great care to speak and write these words with depth, sincerity and seriousness. Not only that, we must also acknowledge the risk involved in theology.

Just as idols become gods, it's possible we can mistake our theology as the full explanation and complete understanding of God. Just as people bow to idols, we run the risk of bowing to our theology.

> It's possible we can mistake our theology as the full explanation and complete understanding of God.

Even when we practice theology with great care, we must remember we might err. We must be willing to hold our beliefs humbly. Just as the people of Israel were influenced by Egyptian culture and made an idol, we too are influenced by our culture when talking about God.

All people who look to the Bible to learn about God do so in a particular time and place. This is why people who are devoted and faithful in their love of God believe different things about him, the church and the Christian faith.

People can read the same Bible passages and come to different conclusions regarding its meaning and implication. This makes things confusing, because those who differ also claim the Bible as their final authority on all things. So when they use the Bible to support their theology, what they are saying seems true even though it disagrees with others.

Of course, this raises questions about the Bible's authority, and how its authority actually works. Who decides how its authority gets applied? Why do some Christians observe one rule for living while others don't? What about the things the Bible does not address? What then is our authority? And if the Bible is to be the final authority, why then is it unclear about so many things?

Answering these questions gets tricky because our answers reveal how embedded we are in our culture and the age we live in. Many of the differences we have regarding the Bible are a result of where we grew up, what faith tradition we identify with and how we have been taught to think. This ought to make us stop and consider how we engage Scripture.

The Bible teaches us about the massive story of God, which invites us to understand this present world and the new world God is bringing about in its midst. We don't merely read the story of the Bible; we, along with God and others, participate in it.

This participation calls us into conversation with God, one another and the Word. It invites us to practice theology—to create new words about God from our experiences with him. The Bible is not something we only look to for theological answers; it also helps us to ask the right questions. It allows us to better understand God, and yet reveals the mystery of God. It causes us to look within to see ourselves as God sees us. Through this, we may find ourselves swept up in the story Scripture tells. When this happens, we discover the deep love of God.

The Bible is a sacred book filled with stories of men and women living in our world. They were just like us. They experienced it all—failure, success, death, birth, betrayal, friendship, love, hate, hope, fear, tears and laughter. Each word offers divine insight, wisdom, instruction and observations about life. One writer in the

Bible even said Scripture is "alive and active. Sharper than any double-edged sword, it penetrates even to dividing soul and spirit, joints and marrow; it judges the thoughts and attitudes of the heart" (Hebrews 4:12).

If Scripture is alive, then perhaps our theology should be too. If it isn't, theology can become static and rigid. But what if we saw theology as alive and dynamic? What if we moved from using theology as an attempt to define God and toward using it to describe God?

DESCRIBING GOD

If I asked you to *define* your best friend, brother, sister or spouse for me, how would you do it? Definitions demand precise meaning composed in concise statements. In some ways, asking you to define a close friend doesn't seem to work. It may serve as a starting point, but beyond that it would fall flat.

If you asked me to *define* my wife, I am not sure I could do it, because applying rigid, exacting words to her would defy who she is in every way. I say this because when we talk about people we love, defining them is not what we normally do, because relationships are dynamic and alive. They are always changing, growing and moving into new seasons.

But if you asked me to *describe* my wife, I could talk all day. And you know where I would start? At the beginning. I would tell you about the first time I saw her. We were both sixteen. We were in our second-period science class, and she sat one row over and two seats behind me. I looked over my shoulder just as she turned and looked at me. The next part is a bit fuzzy, but I am pretty sure REO Speedwagon started playing in the background when we locked eyes for the first time.

I would tell you about our first date, when we watched a firework display while sitting on a bridge, and how I asked her to marry me on that same bridge a little more than six years later. I would gush and laugh and tear up and contradict myself and mess up the order of events that have unfolded in our lives. I would tell story after story of my experiences with her, because in doing so I would describe her to you. And at midnight when you were bleary-eyed and exhausted from listening to me, I would invite you back the next day so I could keep talking about her.

Then I would tell you to talk to her family and ask how they would describe her. I would introduce you to her best friends so they could tell you about her. Through this you would hear different perspectives and learn other stories. In the end you would have a far bigger picture of her than if you just listened to me. In fact, you would learn so much from so many people describing her that in the end you might even feel like you know her.

And you know what? I bet you would want to meet her and spend time with her yourself. Because my wife will always be better than I could ever explain. After hearing so much you would realize what an amazing woman she really is.

What if we spoke about God like this? Not in static but dynamic ways, in ways that led our faith to change and become more robust than ever before? What if theology was our best attempt to describe who God was and is and will be? Would we ever stop talking about him? When we spoke about God, what if we did so in such a way that others began to feel like they know him? What if, after hearing us describe him, they wanted to experience him for themselves?

The biblical writers used all kinds of images and words in an attempt to describe God. Certain descriptions of God in the Bible seem conflicting, other descriptions are downright confusing, but this did not stop the writers from trying to describe God.

The psalmist wrote, "The LORD wraps himself in light as with a garment" (Psalm 104:2). How do we begin to create a mental picture of this? Sure, it's poetry, but really it's an attempt to use words to express something we cannot fully explain.

The prophet Isaiah described God "like a woman in childbirth" (Isaiah 42:14). God is often pictured as a loving mother, one who has given birth to a people. Isaiah later says of God, "you . . . are our Father" (Isaiah 64:8). To be clear, Isaiah speaks of God as both Father and Mother. Which naturally raises the question, Is she our Father, or is he our Mother?

And the descriptions of God don't stop there. God is a consuming fire, living water, a rock, the wind, a tower, love, a judge, a lamb, a shepherd, life, light and a defender—just to name a few. All of these terms are an attempt to explain the God who cannot be explained but we cannot stop talking about. Because sometimes we can talk about something all day, and it doesn't even begin to explain what we have experienced. But we have to say something, because if we hold it in we will explode. This is what the prophet Jeremiah wrote,

If I say, "I will not mention his word
    or speak anymore in his name,"
his word is in my heart like a fire,
    a fire shut up in my bones.
I am weary of holding it in;
    indeed, I cannot. (Jeremiah 20:9)

Like Jeremiah there are some things we simply can't hold in. Maybe this is why the Bible is filled with so many descriptions of God. But why wouldn't God speak clearly and fully explain himself to us? Let's imagine he had done that; would we have any more clarity on who God is? Where would he even begin? How exactly would God explain himself in a way that all humans could grasp?

Some may feel that our descriptions of God leave things wide open, and anyone can describe God however they see fit. But that is not necessarily the case. You see, there are ways of describing my wife that would not be true or accurate. There are things people could tell me about her that I would know, beyond a shadow of a doubt, are wrong.

And as we move to describing God, we will learn he is always bigger than any category we create because we will never be able to fully describe the God who is beyond comprehension. On the other hand, we will find our theology is living and dynamic, just as our relationship with God should be.

We must never forget God is still at work in our world and in the hearts of people like you and me. We still encounter the divine every day. Why then would we think the last word has been spoken? Though God never changes, humans do because our world does, and our faith changes too, which means new words have to be spoken.

We will have no trouble with this because we will never say enough about the wonder of God's presence and our divine encounters in this world. If we commit to faithfully describing God and our experience of him, we just might find God is even better than our descriptions could ever be. This may very well lead us to a place where we are more in awe of God and worship him to a greater degree than ever before.

A theology that does not lead us to worship well could be bad theology. God never asks his people to know twelve doctrinal points with supporting verses. He never commands people to understand him. His call to humanity is simply to come, to trust, to worship and to rest in his love. If we did this, we may develop a far more beautiful theology than ever before.

> **A theology that does not lead us to worship well could be bad theology.**

4

From Words to Experience

■ ■ ■

Words carry meaning beyond their meaning. When spoken, certain phrases, words and names still give me a twinge of pain in my heart and soul. For most people they are mere words, but for me they stir up wounds and memories. These words are worse than sticks and stones that can bruise my bones.

When I was growing up, particular words were used as weapons. They were designed to inflict harm, belittle, insult and antagonize. To this day when I hear someone use these words toward others, it creates all kinds of angst inside me. I want to scream, "Do you know what you are doing with those words?"

I point this out because words are powerful. Ann Voskamp wrote about her friend who often mails books. She wrote, "Every time the postal clerk asks him the obligatory question about if there's anything hazardous or flammable in the package, he always speaks truth: 'You bet—*words*.'"

As a pastor and author I am in a world of words. Most Sundays I stand and speak words to our congregation for thirty-plus minutes. There have been times when some have been moved to tears or laughter when they hear these words. Other times, people have become angry.

Some send emails in response to the words I speak. Some of those emails are filled with life-giving words. Others are littered with words intended to tear down. I can tell you whenever I read these emails in response to my teaching, I feel something inside. Because the words in those emails are not just a collection of letters, they mean something. They have the power to tear down and build up.

We often forget about the power of words because they bombard us constantly. From Facebook to Twitter to blogs to emails, words come at us nonstop. Most of the words we take in are digital and do not feel connected to a person at all. We comment, update, reply and make statements without thinking about our words.

Several years ago I received a nasty email. This went beyond criticism or constructive feedback. The person was clearly angry and wrote it while in a fit of rage. When I received the email I immediately replied using words filled with vitriol and anger. I made sure this person knew he was terrible for sending the email and spelled out in painfully clear detail where he could go and how to get there. No doubt my words would have set this person back a few steps. But just before I hit "send" I remembered advice given to me by a much wiser person.

He suggested when I receive a particularly nasty email, I should not to reply to it. Instead, I ought to invite the person who wrote the email to speak with me face-to-face. Then, when we are together, I should ask the person to read the email out loud. He said, "It will always open a door to good conversation." So, I deleted my toxic response and invited this person to talk.

When we finally met, I brought up his email and asked him to read it aloud. Less than three sentences into the email he stopped. He looked at me and said, "I had no idea it sounded like this. This is awful." The advice I was given proved to be true. From there we had a great conversation. I learned how I had hurt him, which led to him to writing his email. It was no surprise for me to learn I had hurt him with my words.

It's no wonder the Bible is filled with instruction and warnings about the tongue. James wrote, "The tongue also is a fire, a world of evil among the parts of the body. It corrupts the whole body, sets the whole course of one's life on fire, and is itself set on fire by hell" (James 3:6). The biblical writers knew the power of words.

After all, the Bible begins with a poem about a God who spoke words and our world came to be. The first chapter of Genesis is structured around the words of God. Each day of creation begins with the words "God said." Right from the start we learn words have the power to create new things. Abraham Joshua Heschel often told his daughter, "Words create worlds."

This is what the creation poem found in Genesis 1 teaches us. And this is true not only of God's words, it is also true of ours. We have the power to fashion realities, paint a preferred picture of the future and put together new ideas that reshape our world all by using words. My life is different today because of words that created a new world for me.

Shortly after college graduation I was confused and directionless. Not just with regard to life but also with regard to God. He made little sense and the church made even less. One afternoon I sat in friend's office and explained all of this to him. After telling him of my confusion, he stood up, walked over to a bookshelf, grabbed a book, handed it to me and said, "You need to read this."

He then sat down, turned his chair around, faced his desk and stopped talking to me. Apparently he wanted me to read the book right then and there. So I did. Two hours later, still reading, I had learned more about the heart of Jesus than I did in all the years of my life up to that point.

The book? *The Divine Conspiracy* by Dallas Willard.

Within the next few days I finished reading it and had a profound sense my life would forever be different. Willard's book reoriented my life and sent me in an entirely new direction. For the first time I had heard good news that was actually good.

Willard did this with words. And the words in that book created a new world I had never envisioned. Through Willard's words I was introduced, for the first time, to the idea of what we can and should do with our lives. I learned I could have a new, vibrant life right now. Or as Willard called it, "The eternal kind of life now."

We have these experiences with words because of the power they wield. Yet, as powerful as they are, words also have limits. There are times when even the right words cannot communicate everything.

NO HABLO ESPAÑOL

Several years ago my friends Dan and Faith invited me to travel with them to the Dominican Republic. They work in a small, poor community on the shores of Puerto Plata nicknamed Aguas Negras. In the midst of that community is A Light on the Road Church led by Pastor Sandra Tineo.

When I was introduced to Sandra and she heard my last name, her eyes lit up and she spoke to me in Spanish. A little embarrassed I said in broken Spanish, "No, no. No hablo Español." She was bewildered and called to a woman named Sara.

Sandra spoke to Sara, and then Sara said to me, "Your last name is Hidalgo and you cannot speak Spanish?" I explained that while my father is a Cuban immigrant, he never taught Spanish to any of my siblings or me. They both listened, and then Sandra said in broken English with a big smile, "No excuses. You have a good last name. Learn Spanish."

Sara told me she would be with us while we were there and offered to be my translator. She explained she too had a difficult time communicating when she first moved to the Dominican Republic. This surprised me: Sara grew up in Spain and was fluent in Spanish.

"But it's *Spain* Spanish, not *Dominican* Spanish," she explained. When she moved, she presumed the transition would be easy, which is why she was surprised to find few people understood anything she said. The first time Sara spoke at the church she realized that while most in the room understood her words, they did not understand what she was trying to say.

Though she grew up speaking Spanish, she had to learn an entirely new way of using words to explain her thoughts. To do this she first had to understand the Dominican culture, what certain words meant, when to use them and how arrange them in a sentence. Until she did, it was difficult to communicate. Sara grew up learning a language that made sense of her culture in Spain, but those words did not make sense of the culture in Aguas Negras. Even though she spoke Spanish, she did not speak the language.

We use words to express ideas, convey emotions and describe experiences. We use them to understand our world. This is why words can be so powerful. We can use words as building blocks or wrecking balls. Words communicate powerful ideas and have the power to influence thinking, but they also have limits. Sometimes words just don't say all that needs to be said.

> We can use words as building blocks or wrecking balls.

I experienced this recently when I decided to write a letter to one of my lifelong friends on the way to his wedding. He and his wife invited my daughters to be flower girls, and I performed the ceremony. On the flight to the wedding I took out pen and paper to write him a letter. In that moment, a million things went through my head. They were real and heavy and deep, which led me to wonder, *How do I even begin?*

When I am at a loss for words, it's a big deal. It wasn't that I had nothing to write, I had too much to write. I finally began the letter with these words: "At times like this it's hard to know what to say, because there is so much I could say." I wrote him a long letter, and at the end I still felt like my words didn't say anything.

The night prior to the wedding I gave him the letter before he left to go back to his house. The next day he said, "Thanks for the letter. It meant so much. But what means more is to know what a friend you've been and that you are here today." I could have said the same thing about him. His presence as a friend said so much more to me than words ever could.

I am learning that much of the time just being with others is what matters most. My friend Ed says sometimes the most important thing we can do is "show up and shut up." I was reminded of this the other day when I ate lunch with a friend whose brother is dying. He told me whenever he speaks about it, people get uncomfortable and say, "I will be praying for you." He said it's nice people say that, but "they only say it because they don't know what else to say."

This is precisely the problem. In times like these we don't have to say anything. We simply need to sit, listen and grieve alongside others. We need to allow the pain of others to become our pain. Just being there says all that needs to be said.

> We move from human experience toward words, but God moves the other way.

Millions of words will never do what one real experience can accomplish in us. God seemed to know something about this. We move from human experience toward words, but God moves the other way.

SKIN AND BONE

God chose to move from word toward flesh. God knew all the words in the world could never capture who he is. So he abandoned his heavenly world and moved into our world of skin and bones. In Jesus, we see in a powerful way how God showed up to be with us and be one of us.

The apostle John began his Gospel with the words, "In the beginning was the Word. . . . The Word became flesh and made his dwelling among us" (John 1:1, 14). God went from words to human experience. In the person of Jesus we experience exactly what God looks like. This is what Jesus meant when he said, "Anyone who has seen me has seen the Father" (John 14:9). And Jesus did not just come around to live a charmed life. He entered fully into the human experience.

In his letter to the church in Rome, Paul wrote about how deeply God feels with us. His feeling is beyond words. He wrote, "We know that the whole creation has been groaning as in the pains of child-birth right up to the present time. Not only so, but we ourselves, who have the firstfruits of the Spirit, groan inwardly" (Romans 8:22-23). The pain our world feels moves beyond words into an intense cry.

The word that Paul used refers to the cries of a woman in child-birth. It is the kind of groan that expresses pain in a way words never could. It's the sigh we let out and the tear we shed when we hear bad news about a loved one being diagnosed with a terminal illness. It's the moment when we stare at nothing because the pain is so intense that we no longer hurt—we feel numb.

The hope we find in this is that we are not alone. Paul continued, "the Spirit himself intercedes for us through wordless groans" (Romans 8:26). God feels our pain so deeply that he cries out with us. His experience with us is so real words cannot capture it. It's God being there.

Like the Spirit groaning with us, Jesus too joined with us in all our joy and sorrow. There was no part of the human life Jesus left untouched, and this reality has given me much hope. A few years into working as a pastor I hit bottom. I was somewhere between wanting to scream in rage and cry in sorrow.

I did not want to hear any more advice from others, have one more person tell me what God was teaching me, hear how this would help me grow or listen to one more encouraging Bible verse.

Right around this time, my friend Jeff called. Jeff was a pastor at another church, and he knew I was in a rough place.

He invited me to spend some time at his house. It was a cold, overcast day when we met. The weather reflected how I felt. I arrived, he poured me a cup of coffee, we sat down, and I gushed about all the stuff churning in my heart and soul. As Jeff listened, his eyes filled with tears.

After my rant, he leaned back in his chair, looked up at the ceiling and sighed deeply, and when he looked back at me tears ran down his cheeks. I felt such great comfort in that moment, and he did not say a word. Jeff entered into my pain and struggle so much it became his pain and struggle. His tears and silence that wintry day did more for me than words could. Jeff moved from words to experience.

This is why God did not try to explain everything to us. Rather, he entered our world and lived here with us. When we see Jesus, we notice he did not talk about theological concepts, explain God's existence or attributes, and offer clever phrases to those who suffered. Jesus spent his time healing the sick, eating with the outcasts, laughing with children, weeping with those who mourned, living with the poor and ultimately dying for the redemption of all things. Through his actions we understand the unchanging God in a way words could never explain. Because experiences say things words cannot.

> God did not try to explain everything to us. Rather, he entered our world and lived here with us.

We can read about the poor, know the statistics, understand the geography of poverty and know the economic realities that keep some in poverty. But the first time I walked in a slum in Sub-Saharan Africa I learned more about poverty than all the reading I had done. Poverty had a name and a face. It was a mother holding her malnourished son. It was a father dying of AIDS. It was sons and daughters without parents.

This teaches us that our experiences are extremely important. They have an ability to teach us much about God, life and faith. And our experiences inform our words more than our words inform our experiences. Which brings me back to my time in the Dominican Republic.

> Our experiences inform our words more than our words inform our experiences.

Something happened to me while I was there that went far beyond words. I spent the week walking around Aguas Negras with Sandra. I saw the work she and her church do in that impoverished community.

I watched the loving hugs and joyful smiles she gave to everyone she encountered. I saw the houses they built, the families they served, and the men and women who experienced freedom from wretched poverty. I gathered with the community at A Light on the Road Church, listened to them sing in Spanish, watched them sway and dance, and saw the sheer joy on the faces of those in the room. I listened to Sandra preach (in Spanish), and though I could not understand all her words, her presence and passion were uplifting.

What I experienced in my time there was the heart of Jesus being lived out among his people. By the time I left I understood more about those living in Aguas Negras, Sandra, Sara and A Light on the Road Church than I ever thought possible—simply because I was with them. My experience with Sandra and that faith community said more to me than words ever could, and I did not need a translator to understand what it meant.

5

From Knowing to Unknowing

■ ■ ■

Thanks to Google, we now possess the ability to find the answer to nearly any question. For example:

Q: How many dots are there on the original *Pac-Man* board?

A: There are 240 dots and 4 power pellets. Eating these dots slows down *Pac-Man*, so keep that in mind the next time you play the game.

Q: How long will a standard No. 2 pencil last?

A: A standard No. 2 pencil will last long enough for a person to write 50,000 words (roughly the amount in this book), or a line thirty-five miles long. This of course depends on the amount of pressure applied by the person using the pencil.

Q: What is the air-speed velocity of an unladen swallow?

A: Well, this would depend on whether we are speaking of an African or European swallow. In the case of a European swallow, if we factor in wing beats per minute, body weight and amplitude, the average speed would be somewhere between 22 and 24 miles per hour.

Keep in mind, all this data could be wrong, because more than 22 percent of all "facts" are a lie, 16 percent of all statistics are made up, but then again less than 8 percent of the population knows this.

The funny thing is, you could Google every bit of useless information you just read. And even if we did verify this useless trivia, the reality is we are not different or smarter than we were before we began reading this chapter.

Comedian Pete Holmes spoke of our ability to know anything. He said, "You don't know something? Wait two seconds. You will know. Having Google on your phone is like having a drunk know-it-all in your pocket." Google on our phones is "ruining our lives . . . because we know everything but we're not a lick smarter for it. We just know. . . . There's no time for mystery or wonder. . . . The time between not knowing and knowing is so brief that knowing feels exactly like not knowing."

> Google on our phones is "ruining our lives . . . because we know everything but we're not a lick smarter for it."
> Pete Holmes

Holmes is right. We have more access to more information than ever before. While this does have an upside, we forget information is not always what we need. There are some things we can't find the answer to on Google. It may feel like we can know everything about anything, but it's not true. Thinking this way reveals ignorance, not understanding.

When we know very little about something, we tend to think there is really not much to know. It works the other way too. When we know much about something, we know there is much more we can know. This is how I thought about baseball for years.

PLEASE DON'T TAKE ME OUT TO THE BALLGAME

I know very little about baseball, which meant on the rare occasion when I watched a baseball game, all I saw was a guy throwing a ball, someone trying to hit the ball, people trying to catch the ball and others running between bases. How much else could there be? I thought this way until I watched a Major League Baseball playoff game with my oldest brother.

He loves baseball. What I mean is he always wears some kind of baseball-related clothing. When he goes to games, he keeps stats. Every New Year's Day he begins his countdown to spring training. For his birthday two years ago he traveled with me to Phoenix so he could spend two days alone watching spring baseball. His passion for the game is also accompanied with a brilliant understanding of it.

The first time we watched a game I thought we'd mostly sit around, drink beer and talk about life. I was wrong. He was fully engrossed in the game and watched every single pitch. He made what seemed to be very informed comments, which made me wonder if we watched the same game. As much as he seemed to enjoy it, I found it painfully boring. Eventually I asked, "How much strategy is there in baseball?" He looked shock. He tried to look amused, but I think deep inside he was mostly disappointed.

Over the next several months we watched many more games together, and he shared a fraction of his knowledge with me. Every time I learned about one aspect of the game it led me to ask another question. Because the more I learned about baseball, the more I realized there was to know about baseball.

It's like this in life and faith too. The more we know, the more we know there is to know. And we can't know everything.

In the cosmic scheme of things we do not even know a little bit. For example, as much as we know about the ocean, human eyes have seen only 5 percent of it. The smartest doctors and scientists are still trying to understand the complexity of the human brain. And there will always be more, which reveals that we will never know everything. For those of us who prefer certainty, this is troubling. But we must come to terms with our limits.

Just a few months ago I sat with a friend who told me his four-year-old son was diagnosed with cancer. Since then we have prayed for him nonstop. A few times we have gathered to pray over him as we begged God to heal him. Things looked good for a while, and we were hopeful. Then they went back for another scan and received bad news. The cancer has spread, and the prognosis does not look good. The other day he texted me and said, "We know one day he won't be with us, so we are treasuring every single moment with him."

In the midst of this we have asked a lot of questions. "God, why would you let this happen?" "God, are you hearing our prayers?" "God, you have the power to heal, so why won't you?" The difficulty with these questions is there is no good answer. Sometimes God chooses to heal and other times he doesn't. I wish I could tell you why, but I'd only be guessing. I simply don't know or understand, and I'm confident no one does.

When we are confronted with the difficult questions life brings, we are left to wonder. The easy answers don't work anymore, and we struggle to understand. We are forced to move from knowing to unknowing. These are times when we clearly see what we don't know, doubt descends on us, and we ask questions that simply cannot be answered. And this is fertile soil for our changing faith to grow.

DOUBT AS TRUST

Like everyone, I doubt. There have been times when I have doubted God's goodness, love, forgiveness, grace and power. For a long time I did not think I should doubt, and I did all I could to keep it at bay. These days I am learning to no longer lock the door on it but welcome it in like an old friend. Doubt is not the enemy of faith but is essential to it. Doubt is the thing that comes along when we see how little we know. It is the feeling we get in our bones when what we have thought, assumed or believed all along no longer seems right, good or true.

> Doubt is not the enemy of faith but is essential to it.

Before we go any further, it would do us well to define doubt. By *doubt* I mean "strong feelings of uncertainty; something we are unsure of; lack of clarity; or not knowing." Doubt is the big, looming questions we have about God, our beliefs and our circumstances. To doubt is to ask questions in the midst of confusion in an attempt to make sense of our life, faith and God.

I have learned that we all have doubts. This happens because we all believe something about God, life and faith. No matter how firmly we believe these things, what we believe today will be challenged tomorrow, and the answers from yesterday no longer work. We will experience disruption and disorientation leading us into unfamiliar and confusing places.

We should not run from these times but run to them. These experiences have so much to teach us. They are the first step in truly learning something new, not just learning in the sense of gathering more facts or understanding more information. By *learning* I mean being transformed in such a way that we see our world differently and therefore live differently.

When our life is disrupted, when we suffer, when we fall into confusion, we enter a process of doubt in which our way of seeing the world and even our deeply held beliefs no longer work. Then, doubt becomes a wonderful tool for us. But before we can ever use doubt as a tool for learning, we must first admit it's there.

Years ago, before most of us had GPS on our smartphones, we had to write directions to go places we had never been. No matter how clear the directions, I often ended up lost. That wasn't the problem. The problem was I was perfectly content to drive around forever acting like I knew exactly where I was.

On one occasion those with me wore me down and forced me to stop and ask for directions. And where else do you go for directions but a gas station? I explained to the woman behind the counter that I tried to find a friend's house, was lost and needed directions.

She asked for the address I tried to find. When I told her, she looked confused, asked a few questions and then told me I was more than thirty minutes away from where I intended to go. This would not have been a big deal except for the fact my friend's house was only fifteen minutes from mine. I walked back to the car and had to admit to everyone how off course we really were.

But it was not until I admitted I had no clue where I was that I was willing to stop and ask questions. Confusion and doubt are like this. When we are in a place of disorientation, where things are unfamiliar and confusing, doubt asks us to admit that we don't know, which allows us to ask the necessary questions to gain direction in the midst of confusion.

We must learn to give voice to our doubts. One shining example of this in the Bible is Jesus' disciple Thomas. Too often we have spoken of him in a condescending way; we even call him Doubting Thomas. We roll our eyes and sigh when we think of his doubting Jesus' resurrection. But let's not forget Thomas was not the only one with doubts.

Luke, in his Gospel, told the story of the women who went to Jesus' tomb early in the morning. When they discovered he had risen, they ran and "told all these things to the Eleven and to all the others. . . . But they did not believe the women, because their words seemed to them like nonsense" (Luke 24:9, 11). All of the disciples doubted, but only one had the courage to give voice to his doubts.

Thomas heard the reports about Jesus' resurrection, and like the rest of the disciples he doubted. In response he said, "Unless I see the nail marks in his hands and put my finger where the nails were, and put my hand into his side, I will not believe" (John 20:25). A week after he said this he encountered Jesus. One might think Jesus wagged his finger in Thomas's face and said, "Thomas, I am so disappointed. How could you doubt?" But that's not what happened.

Jesus said, "Put your finger here; see my hands. Reach out your hand and put it into my side. Stop doubting and believe" (John 20:27). For Thomas, this was good news. It was Jesus' way of giving Thomas what he needed. Jesus met Thomas in his place of doubt and said, "Thomas if what you need is to put your fingers in my hands, then go ahead." The beauty of this is Thomas encountered Jesus in a way no one else in the Gospels did. Through his doubt Thomas experienced a change of faith.

Sometimes we need to touch the wounds, don't we? Sometimes we need to cry out and give voice to our doubts. Sometimes we need direction in the midst of the confusion.

This is what we find in the book of Psalms, one of the great gifts of the Bible. While it has been the inspiration for countless songs and hymns, more than half of the book is filled with laments. The psalmists give voice to their pain, struggle, suffering and doubt. And they don't go about this politely.

They are angry with God, distressed at their situation and speak from their gut. They say, "Why, LORD, do you stand far off? Why do you hide yourself in times of trouble?" (Psalm 10:1). Notice the accusing tone of the psalmist. He does not ask *if* God is standing far away, he asks him *why* he is standing far away. He doesn't hesitate to lay down his questions before God. He was confused, frustrated and at his wit's end.

Something told him life was not supposed to be like this. God was supposed to be there in times of trouble, and was supposed to stand close to his people. Apparently, God now had different plans and was not acting in the way he should. The psalmist did not give God a pass. Instead, he called him out saying, "God, where are you?" In the Psalms, doubt is not theoretical; it is given a voice and is central to the faith of the psalmists.

> In the Psalms, doubt is not theoretical; it is given a voice and is central to the faith of the psalmists.

They believed doubt and faith worked together to produce something greater. They engaged doubt from a place of faith. This is why we see them crying out to God with their questions. In the midst of their confusion, they believed God may somehow answer them. When we see them express doubt before God, it is actually an expression of deep trust in him.

They trust God enough to rage in front of him and ask probing questions. They knew there is no question we can bring to God that he cannot handle. The psalmists knew they did not know everything, and so they turned, in faith, to the one they believed did know everything and screamed their doubts at him. The psalmists acknowledged they were lost and cried out to God for direction.

NOT THE ANSWER WE EXPECT

Still there are times when our answers are left wanting. We cry out to God and nothing seems to improve. We beg him to restore a life, and he doesn't. What then? There was a man, Job, who experienced this exact thing. He cried out to God, and God answered, but he did not give Job one single answer to any of his questions.

At the beginning of the book of Job we learn he had a wonderful life. He was wealthy, had a large, prosperous family and was "the greatest man among all the people of the East" (Job 1:3). Beyond this, Job loved God. His custom was to offer sacrifices to God for each of his children. He seemed to have it all.

But then things went downhill fast. God allowed Job to be tested, and the evil one took everything away from Job. His oxen and donkeys were stolen, fire burned up all of his sheep, a raiding party made off with all his camels, all of his servants were murdered, and a house collapsed, killing his sons and daughters in a matter of moments. The evil one then struck Job with painful sores over his entire body.

I cannot imagine the pain and anguish Job experienced. Job wondered aloud why suffering suddenly overtook him, and he cried out to God. In the midst of his suffering three of his friends, Eliphaz, Bildad and Zophar, sat with Job in silence and mourning for seven days. Then they made a bad choice and decided to speak.

Throughout the story these three tried to get to the bottom of why Job suffered. They never acknowledged that they did not know everything, nor did they give voice to doubt. They presumed to know it all. They suggested Job sinned secretly, told him he should repent and even pointed out that only fools suffer. Job rightly observed they did a miserable job in their attempt to comfort him.

Job's friends offered answers that did not work. They presumed to know why he suffered and believed they could explain it all. We are so much like them. We still seek to explain why God would allow suffering, and some of our explanations sound like those of Job's friends. We often presume to speak for God as though we can fathom the deepest mysteries with astonishing clarity. Every time we do this, we turn the volume knob of doubt down a little more and miss a chance to learn something by pretending to know it all.

Others offer promises and phrases in an attempt to make suffering sound a bit better. One promise I often hear quoted at funerals and in hospital hallways is everything (including suffering) "works for the good" of God's people (Romans 8:28). It is easy to say these words, but a whole other thing to embrace these words as a satisfactory answer. Because when it really hurts, when taking another step seems impossible, when the wind has been knocked out of our soul and we feel like we are not alive, words—even good ones—can be like knives.

Last year my friend's mother died unexpectedly. Needless to say, it was a dark time for the whole family, but for my friend's father it seemed impossible. His children are grown and married, and he feels alone in dealing with the loss of his wife. I met him shortly after his wife died. We talked for a time, and during the conversation he said to me, "How could God let this happen? And don't tell me this will work for the good or whatever. She was one of the most beautiful, amazing people this world ever knew. How can her loss be good?"

I had no answer. There was nothing I could say. More than that, I agreed with him. I knew his wife. She was generous, loving and caring. Over the course of her life she helped many find sanity and healing in a way they never would have without her. She was young and seemed to have many more years ahead of her. How could this be good?

When I sat with her husband I was broadsided with the fact that nothing could answer his question. No amount of verses, quotes or comforting words would have changed his heart. Some, no doubt, disagree and believe there are good answers, and there are ways of understanding suffering that make sense. They have thought through the problem of pain and attempt to explain suffering in this world in a way that makes sense of even the worst situations. They propose answers to the difficult questions we ask in our dark moments.

Others go the opposite way. They believe there is absolutely no answer that would make sense of a hopeless, painful situation like the death of a good person. They question how a good God would allow bad things to happen to good, innocent people. Or if God really is as powerful as the Bible claims, then why can't he just make the world better. They propose to answer the difficult questions we ask too; it's just their answers are different.

Both those who attempt to explain pain as part of God's good plan and those who argue against a good and powerful God do the same thing. They attempt to answer questions that defy any good explanation. Neither seems content to admit they do not or cannot know. They want to know and try to satisfy themselves and others with answers. But what if God spoke into the situation? What would he say?

When it came to Job and his friends, eventually God spoke. He began with a question and continued to ask questions. In fact, nearly all of his discourse to Job was a series of questions. He began by saying,

> Who is this that obscures my plans
>   with words without knowledge?
> Brace yourself like a man;
>   I will question you,
>   and you shall answer me. (Job 38:2-3)

God asked larger-than-life questions that only the mind of God could fathom. He then said, "Will the one who contends with the Almighty correct him? Let him who accuses God answer him!" (Job 40:2) Job responded by saying,

> How can I reply to you?
>   I put my hand over my mouth.
> I spoke once, but I have no answer—
>   twice, but I will say no more. (Job 40:4-5)

The story of Job is one of deep pain, intense suffering, tragic loss, questions, assumptions and doubt. At the outset it seems the story reveals a lot of answers about suffering.

But the book concludes with God asking questions that are impossible to answer, and the central character, Job, with his hand over his mouth vowing to say no more. And the three presumed intellectual friends of Job look foolish. The message of the book is clear. Not only is it impossible for us to have all the answers, but having all the answers is not the point. It is an invitation for us to move from knowing to unknowing. And when we are willing to do this, we experience doubt as trust.

> Not only is it impossible for us to have all the answers, but having all the answers is not the point.

UNKNOWING IS KNOWING

At the center of the Christian faith is an invitation to know a God we will never fully know. This seeming paradox is what faith is. It is "assurance about what we do not see" (Hebrews 11:1). The Greek word for "see" is also used to speak of understanding. Which means the writer of Hebrews claimed that faith is "assurance of things we cannot understand."

This is the kind of faith we see with Job. He said, "Surely I spoke of things I did not understand, things too wonderful for me to know" (Job 42:3). When Job came face to face with the Almighty, when his eyes had seen God he was overwhelmed by his unknowing. And in that place he rediscovered his faith. Job learned that what he did not know was the very thing that changed everything. As Richard Rohr points out, somehow "unknowing becomes another kind of knowing."

We are good at pursuing certainty and wanting answers, and we have proven we can gather information by the boatloads. But all the information in the world will never explain God. It's not that we can't know God. It's that we can't know everything about God—ever.

Part of me thinks that in the life to come we will not finally know all the answers or be given the ability to fathom all mysteries. Rather, I think for the first time we will finally have eyes to see all we do not know. Which is why we will be able to worship for eternity. In that place we will learn more and more, and in doing so we will discover how much more there is to know. And it will be this way forever.

That's a bit of a mind-bending thought, but one that has an incredible invitation within it. It speaks of a God who wants us to know him, learn from him and trust him. He invites us to ask questions, to express doubts and to wrestle with our beliefs. In this we discover the joy of moving from having everything figured out to staring into mystery and to basking in the awe and wonder of God.

Then we will recognize that each time we participate in wonder, we will rediscover our changing faith.

It's a life in which we can move beyond the small categories we place around God and ourselves, and step into deeper trust in God as we discover his faithfulness to us. A faithfulness that is so true and so enduring that we will never fully know its depths.

6

From Being Right to Being Faithful

■ ■ ■

A few weeks ago I attended a fundraiser for my children's elementary school. Much of the night I sat with two dads talking about anything and everything: marriage, politics, our kids, the Broncos, beer, skiing, poker—eventually the conversation turned to the subject of spirituality. That's when one dad said to me, "I heard you work at a church around here. Are you a pastor?" The other dad looked at me with surprise, like he had just seen Bigfoot.

To be honest, I do not go around trumpeting the fact that I am a pastor. People have had such a variety of experiences with pastors, it often triggers all kinds of responses. If someone asks what I do, I will always share about my work. However, most of the time, I prefer to just be me.

The dad who thought I was akin to Bigfoot said to me, "Does that mean you're a *Christian*?" The emphasis he put on the word *Christian* told me he had some strong opinions that did not seem favorable. He wasted no time in telling me how he grew up in a Christian world, and how he has now distanced himself far from it.

He knew some terrible people who were Christians and others

who were wonderful people who weren't Christians. Then he said, "I have a really hard time believing someday God's going to decide who gets into heaven or who goes to hell based on whether or not they believed the right thing about a few ideas. Like their life doesn't matter." Like him, I have a really hard time believing that too.

I say this because none of us are right about everything, nor are we wrong about everything. But this does raise an important question: What are the right things to be wrong about? Not just the little things but the big, important things. The kind of things that can lead to churches splitting, people leaving churches, pastors writing condemnatory blogs about the beliefs of other pastors, and relationships falling apart. Issues that cause this level of disagreement are not small matters, yet many who passionately follow Jesus disagree on them.

I know people who agree on the person of Jesus and could stand alongside one another and recite the Apostles' Creed with full conviction. Even still, there is one issue they cannot and will not agree on. Their disagreement is so big that in their minds they cannot worship together, because each side believes the other is wrong.

Many of us spend immense time and energy on ensuring we believe the right things about God, life, faith, church, religion and spirituality. We see ourselves as guardians of the truth and believe that truth, by nature, is exclusive. The larger problem is, truth is rarely as exclusive as our claims about what is true.

> Truth, by nature, is exclusive. The larger problem is, truth is rarely as exclusive as our claims about what is true.

Over the centuries men and women have argued for what they believe to be right and are on guard against those they believe are attacking the truth. It's possible, however, in all of this we have overlooked something important in our quest to be right. I'm speaking of the power—or our limited power—of observation, which influences our understanding of what is right and wrong.

THE LIMITED POWER OF OBSERVATION

In the early sixteenth century most people believed earth was the center of the universe. They taught that this is the clear teaching of Scripture and that this view of the universe is *the* biblical worldview. Then a scientist, Nicolaus Copernicus, came along and challenged this widely held notion.

He claimed the earth was not immovable, as many believed. He taught the earth orbited the sun and was in constant motion. Copernicus was nervous about his ideas, knowing many would be against him. He finally published his ideas and died shortly after. But his thinking did not die with him. Decades after the death of Copernicus another scientist, Galileo Galilei, proved Copernicus right.

Galileo used new technology, a telescope, to observe stars, planets and moons. He observed things Copernicus could not see with the naked eye. Even though Galileo had what seemed to be irrefutable proof, he met harsh criticism.

The leaders of the church considered Galileo to be a great threat, accused him of undermining the Bible and charged him with heresy. He was brought before the leaders of the church, threatened with torture and imprisoned. Under these threats he finally and regretfully renounced his theory. He spent the remaining years of his life under house arrest.

Of course, today we know Galileo was right and the church was wrong. Long after the deaths of Copernicus and Galileo, their understanding of the earth and the sun became the accepted and proven way of seeing the world. The power of observation changed, and because of that, what the world believed to be right changed too.

Less than a year after Galileo died, Isaac Newton was born, and his ideas would also challenge conventional thinking and change the way we understand the world. Newton expanded the work of Galileo and proposed ideas about how the world works in relation to energy, motion and the force of gravity. Eventually, his ideas were tested, proven and accepted as laws. His insights and discoveries were held to be true for hundreds of years.

However, unlike Copernicus's and Galileo's theory of the universe, after Newton died his theories were shown to be flawed. Centuries later the theory of relativity expanded the scope of physical conditions, which showed the flaws in Newton's thinking. Newton, as it turns out, was not right about everything. As our ability to observe the universe increased, our understanding of it increased and what was believed to be right changed too.

Centuries after Newton's death another scientist, Edwin Hubble, discovered our universe is expanding. Before this, the scientific community believed our universe was static and unmoving. Hubble's discovery was groundbreaking, but it did not tell the whole story. While he proved the universe was expanding, he and others believed the expansion was slowing down under the influence of gravity. Hubble died in 1953 still believing the expanding universe was slowing down.

Then, in the 1990s three scientists, Saul Perlmutter, Adam Riess and Brian Schmidt, observed something different. They observed distant exploding stars, which led to the discovery that not only is the universe expanding, but also it is continually speeding up as it expands. They were awarded the 2011 Nobel Prize in Physics for their discovery. Their observations changed what scientists believe to be right. Hubble was right about the expanding universe, but was wrong about it slowing down.

Brian Greene brought great insight into how people like Galileo can be labeled a heretic but later be proven right, how Newton could believe he was right and establish theories that are flawed, and how a man like Edwin Hubble can find a startling discovery but not be right about all he observed. Greene spoke at the 2012 TED conference about the power of observation and how it often determines what we believe to be right and wrong.

Greene explained that due to the continual expansion and increased speed of the universe, one day in the future the galaxies we currently see will no longer be visible from earth. The day will come when scientists in the future will observe nothing "but an endless stretch of static, inky, black stillness. And they will conclude that the universe is static and unchanging . . . a picture of the cosmos that we definitively know to be wrong."

He then spoke about those future scientists reading our records based on our observations. They would see we recorded information about a massive universe filled with planets, stars, supernovas, black holes, stellar nebulas and galaxies. Even so, they probably will think we were wrong.

Greene concludes, "would those future astronomers believe such ancient knowledge? Or would they believe in the black, static empty universe that their own state-of-the-art observations reveal? I suspect the latter." Which means their observations will change what they believe to be right, and they will believe we are wrong.

This raises the question, Who is right: we or the future astronomers? Before we quickly jump to say we are right and they would be wrong, let's not forget they would have as much proof as we have. The difference lies in what we observe now and what they will observe then. Because our ability to observe and what we can observe influences what we believe to be right.

And right now, as you read these words, there are things in our world we are unable to observe. There are questions we are unable to answer. If this is the case, how can we know with absolute certainty whether we are right or wrong? And will we be held accountable if we base our belief only on what we have the power to observe or understand? How can we judge something if we can't observe it or understand it correctly?

Like Copernicus, Galileo, Hubble, Perlmutter, Riess, Schmidt and Greene, we are limited in how we observe our world. Newton formed hypotheses, tested theories and made laws based on his ability to observe. The difference today is that our technology allows us to observe the same things Newton observed at a deeper level. Tomorrow we will have technology that will allow us to observe our world in new and better ways than ever before.

Humanity has always observed new things, which has led to new understanding about the earth, the Bible, science, God, the human body and the church. Our new understanding has reformed and reshaped our beliefs about what is wrong and right. This does not necessarily mean everything is changing, only our ability to understand it. And as our understanding grows, it leads to a changing faith. So it is with God—the one who never changes. What's changing is how we understand God. And when our understanding changes, our faith changes too.

All of this makes the question of being right far more difficult than we might first think. Why would we presume we finally arrived at the one place with all the answers for life's difficult questions? Is being right and having all the answers even the point of our relationship with God? When I spoke with those two dads at my children's fundraiser, this was their struggle. In talking to them, I was reminded of two others dads who believe different things about God.

> Why would we presume we finally arrived at the one place with all the answers for life's difficult questions?

TWO MORE DADS

My friend Matt is a pastor, and his dad was also a pastor. His father knew the Bible backward and forward, had a brilliant understanding of the most complex theology, and could debate against the brightest minds in the world. Every week Matt's dad preached to thousands of people, professed his undying love for Jesus and didn't mind people knowing of his near fluency in Greek and Hebrew.

Many people thought highly of him, and he was deeply respected by those in his church. However, behind closed doors with his family it was a different story. In spite of his father's beliefs, Matt told me, "He was a cruel and abusive man." This was not occasional behavior; he was constantly abusive.

My other friend, Jamin, works in marketing, and his dad is a successful businessman. His father has never been interested in Christianity. He's not hostile toward it but has seen the poor way many Christians have treated him and others in business. Because of this, he doesn't believe one religion has the corner on the market when it comes to God, and he feels he is better off without formal religion. He believes in a good, loving God, and has a great respect for Jesus.

He couldn't tell you anything about theology or even name a book of the Bible. But Jamin's dad is one of the most kind, caring, generous, compassionate people you'd ever want to meet. Jamin told me, "I'm not sure there is a better dad out there or a better role model for what it means to be a loving husband."

Matt's father is an abusive person who self-identifies as Christian. Jamin's father is a wonderful person who has distanced himself from Christianity. Some would be quick to point out both of them are wrong about several things, and both will have to answer to God about those things one day. While that's a fair assessment, it still brings us back to the question I asked earlier: What are the right things to be wrong about?

For many, it's repulsive to think that a bad person gets into heaven one day just because his theology is correct. Even worse is the idea that a genuinely kind, loving person is sent to hell forever because he's indifferent to modern, Christian theology. A friend once said,

"That's just the way it is. There will be a lot of good people in hell." So does that mean there will be a lot of bad people in heaven?

Jesus once told a story of two people much like the fathers of my friends. One was considered to be completely wrong about most everything and the other was thought to be right about the important things. As Jesus always did, he upset the accepted, collective thinking.

He told those listening of two men who went to the temple in Jerusalem to pray. One was a very religious man—a Pharisee—who was well-respected and knew all the right things about God. The other man was a tax collector. Tax collectors were considered traitors who were filled with greed and corruption. At the beginning of the story it's clear who is right.

The Pharisee prayed first and said, "God, I thank you that I am not like other people—robbers, evildoers, adulterers—or even like this tax collector. I fast twice a week and give a tenth of all I get" (Luke 18.11-12). Hardly a humble prayer, but really, who could blame him? He had quite a religious résumé. Then the tax collector prayed.

Jesus continued, "But the tax collector stood at a distance. He would not even look up to heaven, but beat his breast and said, 'God, have mercy on me, a sinner'" (Luke 18:13). Jesus then told the crowd that the tax collector, not the religious man, was forgiven by God. The one who thought he was right was wrong, and the one who thought he was wrong was right.

This points to a central theme in the Bible. The biblical narrative constantly teaches we are all wrong, and admitting we are wrong seems to be the one right thing we can do. Still, we pursue being right at all costs.

I know this through painful experience. One part of me loves being right, and the other part of me hates being wrong. I can argue with the best of them. In my worst moments, my ego feeds me lies about why I am right and how I can twist words to prove others wrong. When I descend into moments like this, there is little concern for greater understanding.

My only desire is to appear superior and smart. In these moments I am dead wrong, no matter how articulate my argument. Many of us love to debate our point, prove the other wrong, present opposing ideas and win the argument. From politics to sports to ethics to theology we strive to show the depth of our understanding so we can have the satisfaction of being right.

FAITHFULNESS IS RIGHT

This kind of attitude is what Paul addressed in his letter to the church in Corinth: "If I . . . can fathom all mysteries and all knowledge . . . but do not have love, I am nothing" (1 Corinthians 13:2). Perhaps a modern paraphrase for us today would be: "If I have my doctrinal statement nailed down flawlessly and am able to prove myself right by quoting verses to support my theology, but do not have love, I am dead wrong." We can have all the answers and not be right about anything.

The good news is we can be freed from this constant obsession about being right or wrong, because when it comes to following Jesus, being right is not the most important thing. The most important thing is faithfulness. The division between wanting to be right and committing to be faithful is often a divide between our ego and our soul.

> We can have all the answers and not be right about anything.

Nowhere in the teachings of Jesus does he command his followers to be right, but he does call us to be faithful. Many refer to the Christian life as a "relationship with Jesus." What makes relationships work is not being right but living faithfully in them. Think about our closest relationships, whether it be with a sibling, a friend, a spouse or a roommate.

There are times in these relationships when we miss the point and allow the communication to tailspin into an argument. We try to prove our argument and often stray from the original discussion. We twist words, argue the fine points and allow our emotions to get the better of us—all for the sake of being right. In the end, all we have done is proved we are capable of being unfaithful.

The division between wanting to be right and committing to be faithful is often a divide between our ego and our soul.

Contrast those painful moments with the times we act as a faithful friend, a loyal spouse or a loving brother or sister. We are able to listen, offer caring words of challenge when needed, engage in helpful conversation and cause the relationship to deepen. These are times when we are faithful. And when we live faithfully, right and wrong become readily visible. Faithfulness shines a bright light on that which is good and true.

If this is true in our human relationships, then how much more should it be in our relationship with Jesus? The writer of Hebrews speaks of the countless men and women who were faithful. They trusted God in the midst of trials and uncertainty. The writer concludes, "without faith it is impossible to please God," and they "were all commended for their faith" (Hebrews 11:6, 39). We must learn from them, and move from an ego-driven need to be right toward a soulful desire to be faithful.

This does not mean we give up discussing different viewpoints or working to deepen our understanding of God. But it does mean we should adjust our thinking when it comes to how we approach our relationship with God. We must dig deeper than ever before and always understand we'll never stop observing our unchanging God in new, different and better ways. Through this we will learn how to be more faithful to him.

And this is not easy. It means taking leaps together, trusting in

God's goodness and at times being willing to be wrong in the minds of some. If we do this we will have the freedom to disagree, have varying opinions and will view the world differently. But if we commit to pursuing faithfulness, then our conversations will change. We will no longer strive to be right, but will encourage one another toward greater faithfulness.

In this we will discover we are not the only ones being faithful. Let's not forget, God is far more faithful than any of us. God has always faithfully revealed himself to humanity. Our redemption and the restoration of this world depend far less on us than it does on him. We ought never think our hope depends on our ability to be faithful. Our hope is rooted in God's faithfulness to us.

God is one who continually shows himself to us. As Paul wrote to the church in Rome, "since the creation of the world God's invisible qualities—his eternal power and divine nature—have been clearly seen, being understood from what has been made" (Romans 1:20). Every person who has ever lived has been invited by God to respond to him, and their place in time often determines what their response to his faithfulness looks like. The question for us is, Will we be faithful to how God reveals himself according to our place in time?

THE WA PEOPLE

In his book *Eternity in Their Hearts*, Don Richardson tells multiple stories from cultures around the world who, in observing their world, responded to God's faithfulness. My favorite story from this book is about the Wa people in Burma. Known as a headhunting tribe, they would, each year during planting season, plant human heads along with seeds. They believed this would appease the gods and give them a good crop.

In the midst of this culture, a prophet would occasionally rise up and call the Wa people to repentance. These men were prophets of the "true God" they called Siyeh. They condemned headhunting and the attempt to appease the gods. One of these prophets of Siyeh was named Pu Chan.

In the 1880s Pu Chan convinced his fellow tribesmen to stop their practices of headhunting as other prophets had done before him. In the tradition of the prophets of Siyeh he told the long-standing story of the "white brother with a copy of the lost book." Pu Chan told them if they did not stop, the "white brother" would not come to them for fear of being killed.

Thousands repented and ceased their practices. Then, one day Pu Chan saddled a pony and told his disciples, "Follow this pony. Siyeh told me last night the white brother has finally come near! Siyeh will cause this pony to lead you to him. When you find the white brother, let him mount this pony. We would be an ungrateful people if we made him walk the last part of his journey toward us!"

The pony wandered more than two hundred miles through the mountains, walked into a small town toward a well and stopped. William Marcus Young, a white missionary, was digging in the well. He greeted the disciples of Pu Chan in their language, and, as you guessed, he had the "lost book of the true God." They fell at Young's feet and said, "This pony is saddled especially for you. Our people are all waiting. Fetch the book! We must be on our way!" This story Richardson tells is one of many others just like it.

These stories show us God's faithfulness and his constant willingness to reach out to humanity. But it also says something about humanity. Why is it that over the centuries so many seem to know there is something (or someone) else? Where did the idea of Siyeh come from in the tradition of the Wa people?

As the story goes, Pu Chan and more than ten thousand others from the Wa tribe were baptized and chose to follow Jesus. But what about all those who lived *before* Pu Chan? What about the previous prophets who heard from Siyeh and called the Wa people to repentance? What about the Wa people who in the years before

Pu Chan heard other prophets and repented from their head-hunting ways? They responded to the same revelation Pu Chan and others did. The only difference is they never met the "white brother" or received the "lost book." What about them?

We are left to wonder how high, long, wide and deep is the mercy of God? How far will he go so all might know? Only God himself knows this for sure, but one thing we know is God is faithful to constantly reveal himself to humanity. He has done this so we might seek him and perhaps reach out for him and find him.

This is the faithfulness of God we are invited to respond to. And when we respond to him and live faithfully, we can show all people a better way to live. We then can walk together, arm in arm, with the aim of being faithful, and there is nothing wrong with that.

7

From Power to Truth

∎∎∎

I n war, like everything else, there are always two sides to the story. The difference with war, however, is the side that wins gets to tell the dominant story. As the saying goes, to the victor go the spoils. But the victor also gets something else: the power to determine what is true.

Make no mistake, history is almost always told from the viewpoint of the winner. Most of the story of our world is told by the privileged and powerful who won wars. They control the story we grew up believing. Power fosters the ability to state what's true, and the ability to state what's true creates more power.

My father experienced this when he returned to Cuba forty years after he left. As he spoke with men and women living there he realized they believed a story different from his. Those living in Cuba were told a story by the regime of Fidel Castro. Castro and his side won, and this gave them the power to state what was true for the Cuban people.

> Most of the story of our world is told by the privileged and powerful who won wars.

It did not matter what really happened during the revolution. What mattered was who won, because they became the authors of

the story. They dictated who were enemies, allies, heroes and vil-
lains. In the end, what many believed to be true was the story told
to them by their government. This is not just true in war; it happens
every day in our world.

On cable television alone there are more than fifty channels
dedicated to reporting the news. It doesn't take long to figure out
many of the news outlets are not dedicated to reporting facts but
only what they want us to believe. They can do this, and we believe
them, because they have power. They leverage this power, tell us a
story and call it truth.

It's the same with religions around the world. Priests, imams,
pastors, rabbis, holy books and religious traditions influence billions
of people claiming they have the truth. Some believe this so deeply
they are willing to risk their lives to share the truth with as many as
possible. Others are so committed to the truth they are willing to
fight, kill or die to help others know what they believe to be the truth.

We all have opinions, beliefs, ideas and thoughts we hold to desperately because they tell us a story about our world. We are willing
to defend our truth because something in us seems to know truth
and power are connected. When others believe we possess the
truth, they see us as men and women of power, status and importance. This is why many arguments are not only about truth but also
about power. The problem is many of us misunderstand what power
really is. We believe it gives us a platform to dictate the truth, but
we must learn grasping the truth invites us to let go of power.

This is what the apostle Paul pointed out in his letter to a small,
young church in the city of Colossae. Just like us, they were surrounded by myriads of people who believed the truth to be many
different things.

TOO MANY OPTIONS

Colossae was an important city in the Roman Empire. It was located on the major highway that ran between Ephesus and the Euphrates. The city was known for its expensive wool, which made it a major stop for traders. Being that it was situated on a major highway, it welcomed people from all over the world.

Because of this, there were many different religions and philosophies in the city. And like today, many people were ready to share their opinion of the truth and debate anyone who believed differently. The Christian community in Colossae was no exception to this.

In the city there was an imperial temple for worshiping Caesar, the emperor of Rome. Some believed the truth was that Caesar was the son of god. They sacrificed to him and worshiped him as the human embodiment of god on earth.

Others believed the truth was found in secret knowledge (*gnosis*). They were known as the Gnostics and devoted themselves to understanding the truth. They taught if an individual learned this truth, he or she could escape the evil of the material world and make it into the heavenly realms.

Other religions taught there was a god or goddess for everything. The truth was found in knowing and appeasing these gods so life on earth would be good and prosperous. Just like today, nearly everyone had an opinion about the truth.

These various ideas of the truth challenged the truth held by the church. In his letter to the Colossians Paul addressed this and encouraged them to remain faithful to the truth in the midst of this culture. What's most interesting is what Paul didn't do.

He didn't list the beliefs of others and explain why they were wrong. Nor did he attempt to prove his beliefs were right. He didn't offer a seminar to enable the Colossian church to defend their faith. In fact, he offered very little in the way of convincing proofs at all.

Rather, Paul said his goal is for the church to "be encouraged in heart and united in love, so that they may have the full riches of complete understanding, in order that they may know the mystery of God, namely, Christ, in whom are hidden all the treasures of wisdom and knowledge" (Colossians 2:2-3).

Paul wanted that small church to be "encouraged in heart and united in love." He wanted them to know that all the power on display in the Roman Empire was not what's most important. Of real importance is being rooted in loving relationships with one another. Through this, they will come to know the truth of Christ Jesus. This is his ultimate hope for this church: to *know* Jesus, which is far different than *knowing about* Jesus.

Many of us know a lot about Jesus. As for me, from the day my parents enrolled me in kindergarten until I graduated high school, I attended private, faith-based schools. Every day I heard stories from the Bible and learned about Jesus. I took religion classes, studied the Bible as a part of our schoolwork, wrote papers about doctrine and memorized Scripture verses.

My first year of college I attended a small Bible school where we studied every book of the Bible, not once but twice in the course of ten months. I went on from there to a Christian college, where I graduated with a Bible minor and then on to seminary.

Needless to say, I was around a lot of people who knew a lot about God, Jesus, the Bible, the church and Christianity. After more than twenty years of Christian education, I too knew a lot about Jesus. In my way of thinking, this knowledge gave me power. Not just in my own mind but in the mind of many others.

We believe that knowing a lot gives us credibility, and if we are credible, people will listen to us. And if people listen to us, we will gain influence. And if we gain influence, we will gain power. For too long, I fooled myself into believing this was true. In the end, the power it did yield only served to feed my desire for more power. This kind of knowledge, and the desire behind it, is not what Paul was talking about.

His goal was for them to *know* Jesus. The word he used for "know" speaks of intimacy, not just having the right facts. To know someone meant there was relationship. In certain cases it spoke of such profound intimacy it related to sexuality. This is what Mary, the mother of Jesus, meant when she was told she would have a baby, and she replied, "How can this be, since I do not know a man?" (Luke 1:34 NKJV). Another way of saying this is, "How can I get pregnant, since I've never had sex?"

To know Jesus implies intimacy, love and an intense relationship. This is Paul's greatest desire for the church. But he doesn't want them to merely know Jesus, but to "know the *mystery* of God, namely, Christ." Which raises the question, how exactly does one know a mystery?

> His goal was for them to *know* Jesus. The word he used for "know" speaks of intimacy, not just having the right facts.

A mystery is something that by nature speaks of things that are hidden. It speaks of darkness and unknowing. As confusing as this sounds, this is exactly what Paul means. He wants the church to know something (or in this case someone) that defies understanding. That someone is Jesus.

While this may be surprising to us at first glance, given a little thought it makes a world of sense. Jesus is confounding, shocking and like nothing else we have ever encountered. We need to move from *knowing about* Jesus and move toward *knowing* him. This is something that takes more than a lifetime to learn.

THE MYSTERY OF JESUS

Jesus claims he is the truth (John 14:6), and says he came into this world to testify to the truth (John 18:37). Jesus' claims about himself go beyond words. The truth of Jesus is seen in his life.

It is seen when Jesus touched and healed an unclean leper who knelt before him and said, "If you are willing, you can make me clean" (Mark 1:40). It is heard in his words to a widow who mourned the death of her son when he said, "Don't cry" (Luke 7:13). Truth is in the tears of Jesus who, when he saw those he loved grieving the death of Lazarus, he was "deeply moved in spirit and troubled" and he wept with them (John 11:33, 35). We see truth in action when Jesus, nailed to the cross, cried out to God, "Father, forgive them, for they do not know what they are doing" (Luke 23:34).

This was Jesus' testimony. He was a living example of the truth. More than this, for as much as Jesus claimed to be the truth, he did not pursue power in the way we understand it. He explained this to Pilate at his trial before his crucifixion. He said, "My kingdom is not of this world. If it were, my servants would fight" (John 18:36).

Jesus did not fight, incite an uprising or stir up riots. Jesus, who claimed truth, was willing to give up power, even if it meant going to his death. In doing so, he showed what power really looks like. Power is not found in military might, brute force or brilliant arguments. Rather, it is found in the one who humbled himself and became "obedient to death—even death on a cross!" (Philippians 2:8).

This points to the upside-down nature of the kingdom of God. Those who possess the truth are not on top but often are content to live on the margins. Knowing Jesus, they understand it's not about working our way to the top but to the bottom. This message is found in the Gospels, where Jesus' identity is always in question.

Jesus confounded the religious leaders, and the disciples were skilled at missing the point. Those who seemed to know a lot about God missed the truth of who Jesus was. But some knew exactly who he was, and they are the last people we think would know the truth: a demon-possessed man, a paralytic, a woman with vaginal bleeding, blind men, a pagan woman and the centurion at the foot of the cross.

They understood the truth in a way few did. Many missed who Jesus is because Jesus made little sense to them. This points to the mystery of Jesus. He invites people to full life, but the way to full life is to die. He displays weakness, and in doing so showed us what strength really is. This is seen most clearly through the Eucharist. Jesus told his disciples the bread is his body broken for the world, and the wine is his blood poured out for the world.

The Eucharist is not just a ritual or a simple way of remembering Jesus. It is an invitation for us to participate with Jesus in being broken and poured out for the world. We are invited to participate in the mystery of Jesus. Not just to know it but to live it as he did. To show all people that true life is found in dying to ourselves and that strength is found in weakness. This is the mystery of Jesus of which Paul wrote. It is the reality that in death and weakness we find life and power. Knowing this intimately will radically change our faith.

Paul wants the church to know Jesus so no one will be able to deceive us with "fine-sounding arguments" (Colossians 2:4). Paul invites us to move beyond words, semantics, insights, points and counterpoints, and into a new way of life—a way of life so in tune with Jesus that when others are with us they encounter the truth.

Why? Because it's hard to argue against a true life.

EMBODIED TRUTH

I know a lot of people who love Jesus but have a hard time with the church and religion. Often the divide comes when people see the way Jesus lived, and watch the way many in the church act. While many claim to have all the answers to life's most difficult questions, they seem to know little about the One they claim to follow.

My friend Ben wandered far from the church for years because of the actions of Christians. His father was a pastor at a local church, and eventually was fired. Those who fired him gave no reason, only that there were "issues." As much as Ben's father pressed to understand the issues, it was never explained to him. He was devastated.

A few weeks later, one of the elders of the church called Ben's father. He thought the call was to check in and see how he was doing. He was wrong. The call was to ask if the cell phone he still had belonged to the church. Ben's father assured the elder it was his. The elder thanked him, hung up and he never heard from them again.

In no time, rumors swirled about him. People in the church heard he was an alcoholic or maybe a drug addict. Several people heard on good authority he had an affair with more than one woman. Ben watched his father get beaten up by those who claimed to be Christians. In Ben's mind it did not matter how much these people knew about Jesus, because they did not appear to be anything like him.

How many of us have experienced something like this? Like Ben, many of us have grown tired of fine-sounding arguments, theological debates and another sermon. We have heard people talk for too long, and we want to see real faith in action. We long to see the truth of Jesus embodied. Because, when we see people living like this, something in us knows it's true.

In the second century, Aristides reported to the Roman emperor what he knew about the Christians. He wrote, "But the Christians, O King, while they went about and made search, have found the truth; and as we learned from their writings, they have come nearer to truth and genuine knowledge than the rest of the nations."

> We have heard people talk for too long, and we want to see real faith in action.

His proof that the Christians had found the truth was due to the way they lived. He went on to point out they did not commit adultery, were not promiscuous, were honest, showed kindness and loved their enemies. But he didn't stop there. He spoke of how they cared for widows and orphans, shared what they possessed, took in immigrants like they were their own family, and when someone was hungry they fasted a few days so the needy could have something to eat.

Not one time did Aristides refer to arguments, teachings or doctrine. He knew all he needed to know simply by watching the Christians live. They knew the mystery of Jesus, and as a result embodied the truth.

Fast-forward nearly two thousand years, and the same kind of life is seen in a mother whose daughter was kidnapped, brutalized and murdered. Marietta Jaeger Lane told the awful story of her seven-year-old daughter Susie's murder. She spoke of being filled with rage, wanting to find the one who murdered her daughter, and her desire to kill him. Yet, in the midst of her bitterness and rage, Marietta recalled the love of Jesus and his call to forgive our worst enemies. She chose to yield to the power of God, the One who could reshape her heart.

One year from the day of Susie's disappearance the man who kidnapped and killed her called Marietta's home. She was surprised to find she was filled with compassion for this man. She told him, "You know, I've been praying for you ever since you took her."

How do we argue against that kind of forgiveness? Most of us have done something we regret, and many of us live with the pain of how we have hurt others. We long to be forgiven with such tenderness. Marietta's story speaks truth in volumes to us, because something deep inside each of us knows it's right.

I was moved by this kind of true living by my friend Adam. He told me about regularly visiting a home in Denver for men and women who have experienced traumatic brain injuries. He told me about a man named Rodney who suffered a brain injury that wiped out his memory. Rodney does not know if his parents are alive or dead, he doesn't know who his siblings are, and while he knows he was married, he's not sure what happened to his wife. After meeting Rodney, Adam saw the visitors' log. It was nearly empty. He asked the receptionist if they always have so few visitors. She told him that very few ever stop by.

He then asked about Rodney and the last time he had a visitor. She paused for a moment and said, "No one's been by to see him. At least not since I've worked here."

Adam was in disbelief. He asked, "How long have you worked here?"

She said, "About eight-and-a-half years."

Adam decided this was not right. Even though Rodney doesn't remember Adam's visits, Adam goes several times a month. Because when he is there, as he said, "Rodney knows, at least for a time, someone in this world loves him."

Adam visiting Rodney, just so he knows he's loved, is exactly what the truth looks like. This kind of life testifies to the truth without saying a word, because it doesn't need to. It's the kind of truth one has a difficult time arguing against, because it's a life, not a set of facts or opinions.

This kind of life testifies to the truth in a way words never will. It's moving from talking about the truth and moving toward living the truth. This is why Peter encouraged the church to live good lives in this world. If they do this, even those who accuse them of doing wrong would see their "good deeds and glorify God on the day he visits us" (1 Peter 2:12). Peter's call is for them to live a good life and perform good deeds as a testimony to the truth. By living this kind of life, the church will change the hearts and minds of those who are against them. Peter said this because he knew something in us knows what's true.

A few years ago in Denver several churches came together and created a campaign to address the issue of malaria on the continent of Africa. Out of all the facts presented, the one that persuaded people to give to the campaign was that most malaria-related deaths occur in children under the age of five. People from around the city got involved because they knew what we were doing was right. No one is going to argue it's okay when a five-year-old dies of a treatable, curable, preventable disease.

As human beings we are moved when we see people work for peace, share food with the hungry, use their gifts to serve the vulnerable, give their hard-earned cash so more people can have access to clean water, fight against sex trafficking and care for the homeless. We are moved by these actions because we know they are good and right and true. We must always remember the church is at its worst when it attempts to be the moral police of culture or the enforcer of truth. But we are at our best when we act as a healing agent in our world and extend to all people the loving hands of Jesus.

If we gave as much time and effort in joining God in the work he is doing in this world as we do in arguing with one another, the world would be a far better place. Not only that, far more people may *know* Jesus because they see his way of life lived out by his followers.

I really believe it is that simple.

The prophet Micah said,

> And what does the LORD require of you?
> To act justly and to love mercy
> and to walk humbly with your God. (Micah 6:8)

Leaders in the early church taught the same thing. James taught that true religion is "to look after orphans and widows in their distress" (James 1:27). This is tremendously simple to say, but extremely difficult to live out.

Maybe that's why so many of us are content with merely knowing about Jesus. Because knowing Jesus invites us beyond words into new life and into a changing faith:

> Knowing Jesus invites us beyond words into new life and into a changing faith: a life and faith that embodies the truth.

a life and faith that embodies the truth, testifies to the truth and is the truth in action. If we dedicate ourselves to living like this, we won't have time for the petty arguments anymore, because we, like Jesus, will give our time toward living—really living.

8

From Legalism to Wholeness

■ ■ ■

The night I turned twenty-one, I raised a glass and said to my friends, "To my twenty-first year. May I be drunk more than I am sober." I can't remember what was in the glass, but I know it was gone in seconds. And I never bothered to keep track of how many days of the next 365 I was drunk, but there were many—too many.

During that year it was common for me to wake up with a pounding headache, feeling as though I was ready to vomit at any moment. I would stagger around my house, squinting as the bright light of the morning sun made my eyes throb. I would get to the kitchen, brew some coffee, take a long, hot shower, get dressed, go back for my coffee, sit at my table and spend the next hour reading my Bible and journaling.

You see, while my goal during my twenty-first year was to be drunk more than sober, I also had a fondness for Jesus. I didn't care too much for Christianity and wasn't a fan of the church, but I liked Jesus a lot. It wasn't hypocrisy, mind you; I never told anyone I was reading my Bible. To be fair, I didn't tell many people I was drinking too much either. At that time I was enrolled in a rather strict faith-based college, and it was illegal to drink alcohol. I did all I could to make sure I never got caught.

This was nothing new. I grew up in a world where behavior was everything. Most of the behavior was based on all the things we could *not* do. Which meant, if you were really good at *not* doing certain things, you were thought to be a good, godly person. There were moments when I tried to *not* do the wrong things. My only motivation in those moments was to avoid getting in trouble.

My attempt to obey and follow rules was done out of fear. I was obliged to follow the rules and was told it was my Christian duty to live a moral life. All my tribe seemed to care about was preaching against the evils of sex, drugs and rock-and-roll. This message about morality and obedience was preached so fervently in the world I grew up in that I believed Christianity centered fully on morality.

I heard sermon after sermon about how awful our culture was, how many people are going to hell, what terrible sinners we were and how our culture needs to start living more pure lives. There were people in our church who would go out, stand on street corners with a bullhorn and tell others to repent of their sinful lives.

While I was immersed in this kind of thinking, the message never got through to me. I never cared about the rules or what I was *not* supposed to do. In my mind, if the Christian life was only about morality, then it was not a life worth living.

> If the Christian life was only about morality, then it was not a life worth living.

I say this because of what I saw in the lives of many people who also lived in this world. Like everyone else, we had our personal demons. However, there was no way anyone could ever talk about them. If they did, they would admit to being ungodly and face being judged and condemned by those who kept the rules. So everything in our lives went underground, and eventually our lives fell apart.

This kind of legalistic environment never seems to bring the best out in people—just the opposite. Legalism is a checklist, a rulebook and a bullet-point outline of how one can live a God-pleasing life. The exacting demands and pressure placed on everyone is anything but life giving. It's a slow, painful death, with Jesus' name wrongly stamped on it.

The reason it is so lethal is because it lacks soul. In those days I rarely heard anything about joy, peace, grace, mercy or love. It was an empty religion devoid of life, with an emphasis on sin and death. We were routinely told our sin makes God angry—this kind of thinking is a gross reduction of the Christian faith. Like many, I figured out it wasn't working, and I decided it wasn't for me.

THE OTHER SIDE OF THE SAME COIN

When I tell people about the world I grew up in, most are in shock. They cannot fathom going to a Bible college that was so strict. Today, most people I meet see beyond narrow rules and recognize that things which may have mattered yesterday are unimportant today. Though we may see beyond narrow rules, it's possible we are still living the same kind of lives today.

Of course, we don't care so much about trivial rules, nor do we focus on what people should *not* do. But we still have rules and demands we place on people—they are just a bit more appealing and more in step with our world today.

Many Christians have rediscovered God's heart for the poor and our call to be peacemakers. In our churches today we hear sermon after sermon about how broken the world is, how unjust it is that so many people are suffering—lacking access to clean water and proper nutrition, and having no life-saving medications—how abused our environment is, and how we need to act to restore and renew our world.

Many have sounded the call to Christian communities to join with God in his mission; some even use the term *missional* in an attempt to define the kind of life they live. Books have been written, conferences have sprung up and blogs have been created, all with the aim of learning to live a missional life.

Don't get me wrong, it's wonderful to see many reawakening to God's love for the marginalized and reclaiming our call to care for the earth. We need to keep turning up the volume on this. But if this is the only song we play, we are in danger of once again doing nothing more than giving people rules to live by.

If we are not careful, we may move from a culture that told us all the things we should *not* do to one that tells us all the things we *should* do. It's just more rules to be obeyed, and we may find people believing that if they are good at doing certain things, they are then good and godly. Being missional can become nothing more than a new form of legalism.

I recently read an article written by a pastor on his decision to shift his church toward being more missional. He had plans, classes, illustrations and a series of sermons designed to get people out of the pew and into their world. While this is good, it boiled down to outlining new rules to follow.

> Being missional can become nothing more than a new form of legalism.

On one hand, it is hard to argue with this. When it comes to new territory or new thinking, we often need very clear-cut directions and understanding. However, the problem lies with what people have experienced in the church over the last century: legalism. For so long we have been told the rules and given a checklist that gives us security in knowing we are doing the right thing. Today, many have exchanged the demand to be moral for the demand of being missional.

However, we can be extremely moral and missional but become nothing more like Jesus. We completely miss the point as long as we follow rules out of obligation. At the end of the day we will continue to feel empty if we are only roused to action because of an exciting event or feeling guilty about not doing enough. All of this is mere legalism as long as we ignore what is central to the Christian faith—a transformed heart. We need to move from legalism and move toward transformation.

This is no small thing. When Jesus spoke about transformation he did so in terms of death, resurrection and new life. In one conversation with a man named Nicodemus, Jesus talked about transformation as being "born again."

Nicodemus was a well-respected, influential religious leader who sought out Jesus. Jesus said to him, "No one can see the kingdom of God unless they are born again" (John 3:3). Nicodemus, a little confused by what Jesus said, asked, "How can someone be born when they are old? . . . Surely they cannot enter a second time into their mother's womb to be born!" (John 3:4). It may have been an attempt at humor on Nicodemus's part, but Jesus repeated what he said about being born again.

Jesus revealed how massive and reorienting this transformation is for us. Following Jesus is not about having a checklist; it involves a complete reorientation to the world. He invites us to experience a changing faith, an entirely new life that Jesus compares to childbirth. Paul says that the individual who experiences it is a "new creation" (2 Corinthians 5:17).

This is far more than doing a few things, obeying a few rules or behaving correctly. The transformed life is brand new territory. Jesus is more concerned with who people are, not what they do (or don't do). He knows that when we live out of a transformed heart, morals and mission will take care of themselves.

IT STARTS HERE

Rules, guidelines and staying busy cover what may really be going on in our lives. I know this about myself. This is why for most of my life I did not want to look inward, because I knew what was in my heart.

One beautiful summer evening, however, I came face to face with what was inside. My wife and I went out for dinner. As we spoke, she brought up the name of someone who had caused tremendous pain in my life.

The longer we spoke, the more agitated and angry I became. It's hard to explain, but when anger is deep inside and begins to come out, you almost sense yourself becoming physically stronger. In the middle of our conversation my wife looked me deep in the eyes and said, "You are really angry."

It wasn't an accusation or a casual observation. It was a statement from a person who loves me deeply. She spoke out of her pain for me. She was not trying to fix anything but wanted to help me see what she saw. Her words went straight to my heart, undid every defense I had and unearthed deep wounds inside me.

For the first time in my life I listened when someone told me I was angry. There had been multiple times before where someone would yell at me and tell me I was an angry cuss. But this was the first time anyone told me so candidly and lovingly. She was right, and it meant things had to change. I had to get behind the anger and expose the very thing causing my temper—a bruised, wounded heart. I realized in order to get rid of my anger I had to go into my heart.

Over the next months I explored my heart, and it was terrifying. At every turn there was hurt, pain, fear, mistrust and heartache. Not only mine, but pain I had caused others because of my anger. Things got worse before they got better because of all the dark stuff I kicked up that had lingered inside for years. The further I went on my journey, the angrier I became. But eventually my anger began to diminish.

My journey into what seemed to be just a bad temper from a hotheaded kid proved to be so much more. I confronted sorrow, loss, wounds, shame and abuse. I confessed self-loathing and recognized how I lived rooted in fear. I came to grips with the fact I had wounded a lot of people in my life—people I dearly love—and it was time to ask forgiveness.

Even though the journey was difficult, it was also beautiful. For on this journey I met God. I did not begin searching for God, but it would have been impossible not to see him. It seemed as though he was everywhere: in every hurt, in all my wounds. He was in the middle of it the whole time. This God was not far away from me in my times of pain; he was closer than the pain itself. Close enough to feel it with me.

He is not a detached God who looks at our wounds and thinks, *Why, that's horrible!* He is a God who was wounded for us and with us, a God who carried the cross and took our shame. He is found in our pain. This is the reason we so often encounter God in the midst of brokenness. It is from this place that he brings us healing, wholeness and hope.

I learned this through my journey of healing, and I saw firsthand how God transforms even the most broken, messed-up hearts. And I'm still learning this every day. This is where we need to begin—not with all the rules or all the things we are supposed to do and not do. We need to begin with our hearts. Looking inside must always come first, because without a transformed heart, our encounter with God would be too much for us, and any attempt to serve our world would fall flat.

Perhaps, like me, you find the idea of looking honestly at your heart terrifying. Maybe you've been told you're beyond hope. It's possible you think you are too broken to ever be repaired. No matter where we are, the good news is none of us are beyond God's love, hope and grace. We all are invited to move from brokenness toward healing. Even in the darkest, most broken places in your heart, God can and will do something new.

> Even in the darkest, most broken places in your heart, God can and will do something new.

THOSE AREN'T JUST ANY TREES

When God led the people of Israel out of slavery in Egypt, he promised to lead them to a land inhabited by a people called the Canaanites. The Canaanites were famous for their military strength, their culture and their wealth. Their fertile land allowed them to have a surplus of food, livestock and money. They believed they owed their success and blessing to the gods, who they worshiped with devotion.

As God prepared to lead his people into the land of the Canaanites, he wanted them to steer clear of Canaanite gods. When they got into the land, God told his people to tear down the Canaanite altars, destroy their idols and "cut down their Asherah poles" (Exodus 34:13). Asherah was a fertility goddess widely worshiped in Canaan. In Hebrew "Asherah pole" means "trees" or "groves." Asherah was associated with oak trees.

God told the people of Israel to go into the Promise Land and cut down trees. He told them this because trees were connected to primitive religious practices. The ancient people believed trees were both divine and earthly. Those in Canaan thought large, old trees were cosmic—some even believed them to be trees of life. They were a bridge between the human and divine realms.

These trees and groves were the first temples of the gods. Under these trees people built altars, fashioned idols and participated in rituals. Their activities under the oak trees was so dark some historians won't record what happened. The trees gave cover and allowed worshipers to participate in those dark acts without anyone seeing what they were doing. It's no wonder God told his people to cut down these trees and smash the idols.

But the Israelites did not listen. They saw the fertile fields in Canaan and learned that Asherah gave abundance to her people. Life depended on good crops, and the people of Israel believed if they did not worship these gods there would be famine and death.

So why risk it? They didn't want Asherah upset with them, so they joined in worshiping her.

It was not just the everyday, ordinary people who did this. Several kings of Israel also worshiped Asherah. This became so engrained in the life of so many people that the prophets cried out against it. The prophet Isaiah said, "You will be ashamed because of the sacred oaks in which you have delighted" (Isaiah 1:29). Isaiah informed the people that all they'd done beneath those trees was going to be brought to light. Can you imagine what it would have been like to hear those words?

Many of us have a dirty, little secret. We've prayed for forgiveness over and over, but no matter how much we pray we never feel like God has really forgiven us. We've done all we can to forget about it and cover it up. It nags us and is eating us up from the inside. Imagine how we would feel if someone told us they knew about it, and it was going to be made public? What would we do?

This is what Isaiah told the people. He knew they burned "with lust among the oaks, and under every spreading tree" (Isaiah 57:5). They ignored their hearts and abandoned their God. It's tempting to look back at these ancient people and think we have come so far today.

All that has changed, though, are the things we place our trust in. For the ancient people it was trees, myths, gods, idols and super-stition. For us it's education, money, empires and religious systems. One thing that has not changed is our tendency to ignore our hearts and pursue something other than the God who wants to heal and transform us. When we read the words of Isaiah, we should read them as though they were written for today.

If we do, however, we must read more than the few verses about how terrible things have become. We may think the next few verses record how God was going cut down the oak trees himself, and would punish and destroy the rebellious people. But that's not what God says.

Instead, God tells his people things will change, that good news is on the way. He promised that the brokenhearted would be healed, the captives would be freed and the prisoners would be released from darkness. God would forgive all they had done, comfort them and provide for them. He would,

> bestow on them a crown of beauty
>   instead of ashes,
> the oil of joy
>   instead of mourning,
> and a garment of praise
>   instead of a spirit of despair.
> *They will be called oaks of righteousness,*
> a planting of the LORD
>   for the display of his splendor. (Isaiah 61:3, italics added)

Wait, what? Now God is talking about planting oak trees? This may not be the best word picture, right? Actually, just the opposite.

In the place of their greatest failure, deepest regret and worst mistakes, God told his people he would plant something new, and something beautiful will grow from it. In other words they will tell a new story. God told the people their story does not have to end this way. No matter what happened yesterday, regardless of today, tomorrow can be different.

God wanted his people to experience deep, true, lasting transformation. That has never changed. This too is what he wants for us today. These verses from Isaiah 61 are the same ones Jesus read aloud in a synagogue. When he finished reading these verses he said to those in the room, "Today this scripture is fulfilled in your hearing" (Luke 4:21).

Jesus wanted us to know we are never beyond repair. In effect, Jesus says to us, "In the place of your worst failures, your biggest mistakes, your greatest shame, your dirtiest secret, your failing strength, your deepest wound, your messiest sin and devastating brokenness, I will plant my seeds of love, grace, compassion, hope, mercy, wholeness and healing. And in that place something new will grow that will put my splendor on display in you and through you so that the whole world will know that our stories don't have to end with ashes and mourning and despair. I am the One who rebuilds, renews and restores the places that have borne memories of grief and sorrow."

My friend James lived for years believing he was beyond repair. As he tells it, his life was a lie. He was always the good kid, the golden boy who could do no wrong. He knew what *not* to do and what he was supposed to do. He was an expert at managing external appearances. He killed his own emotions, never got mad or upset, and was always the life of the party. As an adult a sinking feeling overtook him. He realized he had no real friends. No one knew him because he always kept his dark secrets hidden.

James's past involved sexual abuse as a child, which destroyed not only his innocence but a proper understanding of sexuality and healthy relationships. He tried to bury the abuse through multiple relationships with women. After he married, the pain was still there. He developed another relationship with a woman that led to an affair. The more he ran from the pain, the more pain he caused.

Years later the pain was too much and he knew he had to turn and face it. He told his wife, his friends and eventually, at his own choosing, he met with the leadership of his church. When he told his story to them he could not believe their response.

They wept with him and his wife. They prayed over him and walked with him, step-by-step, over the next two years toward healing and wholeness. He told me he never experienced anything more powerful in his life.

James discovered that transformation could not happen outside of his pain but right in the middle of it. He found God in the midst of his wounds and the mistakes. Right in the middle of his mess, God planted something new, and it has grown into something beautiful.

WHERE WE BEGIN

It's tempting to concern ourselves with religious obligations or focus on what we are supposed to do for others in the name of Jesus. When we get caught in this trap we become defensive when others talk about change, and even combative if someone talks about a changing faith. If all we have are a few *oughts* and *shoulds* as the foundation of our faith, any talk of change can cause things to fall apart.

If our faith is centered on how we perform, we will overlook what God wants to do in us and for us. It's not about the rituals or traditions or rules, but what's inside us: namely, our heart. Many of us know our hearts are messy, dirty and riddled with scars and shame.

> If our faith is centered on how we perform, we will overlook what God wants to do in us and for us.

It's so easy to cover it up and not disturb it. But this is exactly what propels legalism. Legalism allows us to perform without questioning what's inside. So we get busy doing all sorts of things and ignore our hearts, but when we ignore our hearts whatever is there doesn't go away. It festers and grows, and at some point it will spill out.

We can say and do all the right things, be missional and act out a beautiful spirituality, but in the end these may only mask what's inside. This is why Jesus called some people hypocrites. Hypocrites were actors in the theater who wore masks. Their masks bore exaggerated features so people could tell what kind of character they represented. Yet, people never knew who the actor was behind the mask.

When it comes to acting, what matters is the mask. When it comes to legalism, what matters is the performance. But when it comes to Jesus, what matters is the heart.

In the church, the more we are told to "not do" or to "go and do," the more danger there is of overlooking our hearts. If pastors insist we obey rules or be more missional, we may miss the transformative journey. It's easy to do. A clever trick of the evil one is getting the people of God to do a lot of things that are good and right so we fail to see the *one thing*: transformation. Here's the irony: while we can be more moral and missional and not become more like Jesus, we cannot become more like Jesus without being more moral and missional.

God does not ask us to have a checklist. He does not demand we do certain things so we can feel good about ourselves at day's end. He invites us to move from being consumed with doing and not doing, and move toward deep and true transformation so we can experience a faith that changes us. The spiritual journey always begins by fearlessly looking within our hearts. For when we do this, we

> We can be more moral and missional and not become more like Jesus.

will understand who we are. Then we can discover the joy of joining with God in his work in this world.

9

From Toil to Work

■■■

When I graduated from college I had a bachelor's degree in communications and zero life direction. My professors told me I could do whatever I wanted with a well-rounded degree like mine from a liberal arts college. The problem was, I did not know what I wanted. My first job out of college was working second shift at a factory assembling large conveyor systems for baggage claims at airports.

I was miserable. Every day I woke up, looked at my watch all day and felt like I sat around waiting for work to start. The work was lonely. Everyone in my area of the factory worked at his or her own bench. Between the noise of the drills, machines, factory cranes and wearing earplugs, it was complete isolating. I am an introvert, but this was too much.

The money was good, but no matter how big the paycheck, nothing could make my situation better. I hated my job. Everyone I worked with hated their job too. On our breaks we would talk about what we would do when we no longer worked at the factory. These conversations led me to a moment of clarity.

I didn't so much hate my job as I hated the fact that my life lacked meaning. I could have worked ten other jobs and felt the same way.

I was miserable because I had no idea what I wanted out of life. I felt like my life didn't matter. What I mean is, if I had died back then I'm not real sure what people would have said at my funeral.

Of course, they would have said nice things because that's what you do at funerals. However, it would have been hard for them to keep a straight face. Sure there would have been funny stories to tell or nice anecdotes from my siblings about what kind of brother I was. But I wanted something more out of life, and not just for me.

I wanted to know I would make a difference in the world and in the lives of others. A few months after starting my job at the factory I asked myself what I planned to do with my life. I knew there was something more, but I struggled to know what that was. Then something unexpected happened that proved to be a hint to what I would do with my life.

My friend Dan, a youth pastor at a local church in town, asked me to join his team as a volunteer in the middle school student ministry. Most Sundays I showed up to hang out with the students, which was comfortable enough. All that changed one morning when Dan called.

I was on my couch and didn't get up when I heard the phone ring on my spray-painted-blue, synthetic wood table. The answering machine picked up the call, and I listened as Dan left a message. His voice echoed off the walls and wood floors of my scarcely furnished apartment. He chatted for a time, almost like he knew I was listening.

Then he said, "I need you to teach the students this Sunday and speak about why Jesus came to us on this earth." He didn't really ask me if I would, which made me feel like I couldn't turn him down. My only confidence was my communications degree. I could do anything I wanted with that degree (ahem). Before I left for work that afternoon, I called him back and uneasily agreed to teach the students. It was Tuesday. I had four days to prepare something.

The next morning I found a stately volume of theology, read a few pages, organized my teaching into three points and finished it off with a riveting conclusion. I met with a friend, a teaching pastor at a church, and proudly presented the outline of my masterpiece. He read it over, winced, looked at me and said, "If you preach this to the middle school students, they will laugh you out of the room."

At least he was honest.

We spent the next few hours together, and he helped me construct a teaching. The next day we did more of the same. I took all of my notes, wrote an outline, and together we walked through it on Saturday. Before I left, he smiled and hugged me. It like the kind of hug you give to someone when you know something bad is going to happen.

Sunday morning came. I stood to teach and saw hundreds of middle school students staring at me, begging me to say something they could bear listening to. I stared back at them, knowing my college degree meant nothing. In that silent moment, which was both a second and an eternity, I began to speak from somewhere I never knew existed.

Something in me wanted everyone in the room to learn what I had learned. As I kept talking, this deep sense of truly living came to me. That day when I left the building, I got into my car, and my future wife said to me, "That was the most *you* you have ever been." She saw what I felt, and I knew it was right.

The following week I hung out again with my teaching-pastor friend. He asked how the teaching went, and as I began to talk about it my knees bounced in excitement, I spoke faster and faster, and I was nearly out of breath. He smiled and said, "I knew it. God has hardwired you to teach."

Over the next months and years I spoke anywhere anyone would have me. From rehabs to high schools—it didn't matter. Something was given to me, and I lived to give it back. Given the chance, I think I would have spoken to animals in a petting zoo. Teaching became the one thing I could not stop doing. I still worked at the factory, but for the first time I realized my work and my job were two different things.

IT'S (NOT) SUPPOSED TO BE LIKE THIS

When I talk about work, I am not talking about the thing we do because we *have* to do it or get *paid* to do it. The way we understand work is not the way God intended for us to live. This is why work is drudgery for so many, and why we hated our factory jobs. Genesis calls this "painful toil" (Genesis 3:17). Unfortunately, we have given so much of our lives to this, failing to see it makes us less human.

In our toil, we strive to make the best and most products in the shortest amount of time for the least amount of money. We are consumed with productivity and efficiency. Books and seminars and bloggers share advice on how to work harder, faster and smarter.

However, productivity and efficiency were first associated with machines, not humans. These terms were applied to humans after the introduction of machines into the workplace during the industrial revolution. Machines were productive and efficient in a way the world had never seen.

> Productivity and efficiency were first associated with machines, not humans.

Eventually the line was blurred between humans and machines; both were seen as tools to get work done. Like machines, humans became dispensable parts of the operation. If one breaks, get a new one that can do the same thing—only better, faster and cheaper.

While this may work in relation to making parts for cars, it should not be the way we think about human lives, but it has become normal for many of us.

It is any wonder so many people hate their jobs? We are engaged in toil. As the Teacher in Ecclesiastes taught, "The toil of fools wearies them" (Ecclesiastes 10:15). More than stealing our humanity, it dangles the promise of meaning in front of us, but always fails to deliver on its alluring promise. We are addicted to this.

This is why so many people are workaholics. I recently spoke with a man from our church who told me he cannot stop working. He sounded like someone talking about drug or alcohol addiction. He needed more and more to get the same high he got early on. It was eating him from the inside out. Toil promises everything and delivers nothing. Indeed, "toil is the misery of man."

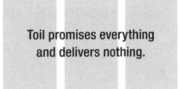

Toil promises everything and delivers nothing.

For much of our life, toil is all-consuming, but at the end of our lives it will leave us empty. It's chasing after the wind. It's meaningless. At the end of our lives none of us will say we wish we had spent more time working for our company or brokered just one more business deal.

Meaning will never be found in toil, but we can't say the same thing about work. Work is part of what it means to be made in the image and likeness of almighty God. God called us to this from the very beginning; the question is whether we will hear his call to move from toil and toward work.

When I talk about work, I'm talking about our calling or our *vocation*. The word *vocation* comes from the Latin work *vocare*, which means "to call." Frederick Buechner said vocation is "the place where your deep gladness and the world's deep hunger meet." I can't think of a better way to describe work. When we engage in work like this, we become more human.

The first thing we learn about humanity is we were invited to work with God in his good world. Genesis says God put the first man "in the Garden of Eden to work it and take care of it" (Genesis 2:15). This was their calling, and it is the same for us today.

The biblical story of humanity began in a garden with gardeners working with God. This call to work was renewed in Jesus. In John's Gospel, when Mary Magdalene first saw Jesus after his resurrection she thought he was a gardener (John 20:15). This is more than a passing detail.

A new story about a new humanity begins with Jesus recognized as a gardener in a garden. As followers of Jesus, like the first man and the first woman, we are invited to work with God in this good world. We are invited to work toward something greater than ourselves. This work gives us meaning.

God wants us to work with him in the renewal, redemption and reconciliation of the world. This is why Paul wrote we have been given the "ministry of reconciliation" (2 Corinthians 5:18). Now there's that word *ministry*.

Too often we have been led to believe that ministry is "sacred work." We speak of those who work in a local church as being in "full-time ministry." Many believe that working as a pastor or a missionary is more sacred than working as a waiter, a CEO, a bus driver or a salesperson. This belief is toxic.

In the midst of our changing faith, we must reclaim what it means to be ministers. This begins by moving from toil toward work. My friend Jeff once said the reason he loves our church is because on Sundays the "ministers are the ones sitting in the seats in the auditorium, not just the person standing on the platform." Jeff's changing faith has led him to see that calling is not only for men and women who work at a church, for a nonprofit or serve as missionaries.

All of us have a vocation or calling. As a pastor, many have said to me, "Tell me about your calling." And I always do, but then I ask them to tell me about their calling. Nearly every time the person says, "Well I'm not in ministry." But that simply is not true.

It's tragic to believe we have little to offer this world because we believe our work is not sacred. Remember, when speaking about work we are not talking about our jobs but about the ministry of reconciliation God has given to his people. It's no small thing either, because God is reconciling "to himself all things, whether things on earth or things in heaven" (Colossians 1:20).

We instinctively know this. Eternity has been placed in our hearts, which is why something inside us is screaming to live

> It's tragic to believe we have little to offer this world because we believe our work is not sacred.

beyond the borders of our skin. Vocation is the call inviting us to do just that. All of us have an opportunity to work and experience a life that matters.

WHAT SHOULD WE DO?

At the end of Matthew's Gospel Jesus told his disciples to "go and make disciples" (Matthew 28:19). This command was not for them only. It's for all of us. It's Jesus' invitation to continue the work he started when he walked on this earth.

We may hear his words and think, *Do I have time for this?* We wonder where in our busy schedules we would fit one more event or appointment. From Sunday morning worship services to "quiet time" to mission trips to weekly small group meetings, we often think of our faith as a series of events.

On top of our commitments at a local church, we have our job, friends, family, exercise, sleep and so on. Time is a precious, non-renewable resource. Jesus didn't want his disciples to schedule time to do more, but to learn to see the world with new eyes.

After Jesus gave them this command, they went back to Jerusalem and continued to live as they always had. They had the same daily routines, lived among the same people and made their daily trip to the temple for prayer.

In the book of Acts the writer describes the life of the first disciples and the early church saying, "All the believers were together and had everything in common. They sold property and possessions to give to anyone who had need. Every day they continued to meet together in the temple courts. They broke bread in their homes and ate together with glad and sincere hearts" (Acts 2:44-46). At first glance there was nothing abnormal about being together, sharing possessions, looking out for one another, meeting daily in the temple and sharing meals. This is the way a family would have lived in first-century Jerusalem.

But this is also unusual. Acts 2 is not describing a family but a group of men and women from all walks of life who chose to live this kind of life together. At the center of this new community were the disciples, who invited others into their life. They didn't do more or add more to their schedule, rather they approached their daily routine with greater intention and purpose. It's no wonder more people were added to their number everyday (Acts 2:47).

When we think of our work, we must move from wondering about the time commitment and toward joining God in working toward the reconciliation of all things. We must learn to see all the ways we can be a part of this, not by doing more but by seeing things differently. In our day-to-day lives we encounter many people in need of God's love, grace, mercy and restoration. The question is, will we do something?

Our work is not limited to any one place. It's done in our neighborhoods, at our local schools and places of employment, with our family, at our local churches, and in our communities. Our work is to bring light into the world and be a part of the reconciliation of God wherever we are. It's not doing more but learning to see what is directly in front of us.

In time we will see everything we do is sacred because it is working with God as his ministers in this world. Bono is quoted as saying, "My position is that I write songs, I'm in a band and I hope that when it's all over for U2, that in some way we made the light a bit brighter. Maybe just tear off a corner of the darkness." For Bono his life is not about the music or the band. It's really about tearing a corner off the darkness. That is sacred work. When we do

> Our work is to bring light into the world. It's not doing more but learning to see what is directly in front of us.

this, we call attention to the light, and even the darkest places become holy. We can help others see the presence of God that has been there the whole time. We can wake up to the fact that the ground is holy. If we hear the call of God and work with him, we will wake up to see his goodness everywhere. And we will help others wake up too.

IT'S ALREADY THERE

Last summer my family and I went for a walk early one evening. My son was on his bike, my older daughter was on a scooter, and our youngest daughter was in a stroller. I was pushing the stroller watching my two older kids race down the street, feeling relaxed and not thinking about much, but that all changed in an instant when I smelled burgers cooking.

Up to that point I did not even know I was hungry since I had just eaten lunch a few hours earlier. Now, my mouth was watering. I kept commenting on how good the grill smelled, so I started making plans to go to the store, buy some meat and grill burgers. It was almost all I could think about.

When we got home I grabbed the keys and drove up the street to our neighborhood grocery store. I bought all I needed, drove home, fired up the grill and threw the burgers on. We set the table on our patio as the burgers finished up. I sat down, put my burger together—bun, meat, bacon, avocado, cheddar cheese, mayo, lettuce, tomato—took a bite and said, with my mouth still full, "Tchzis dase soo goo" (this tastes so good).

Let's not forget, just ninety minutes before, I was on a walk with my family, not thinking about grilling or eating burgers. This raises the question, how did I go from contented family man on a summer evening's walk to having an insatiable need for burgers? Simple.

The cooking burgers awakened something inside me that revealed my hunger. It had been there the whole time; I had just missed it.

This is what we do in our world when we tear off a corner of the darkness. We shed light in places revealing what had been there the whole time. Our work acts as signs for others about what our world is really like; it helps them understand where they are and reveals where they are going.

This is the kind of life I have witnessed in my friend Pamela. Everyone that knows her loves her. And it's not just because she's funny, kind, intelligent or generous. She *is* all those things, but they love her because everywhere she goes she brings light and life with her.

Pamela is an attorney who works with the Justice and Mercy Legal Aid Clinic in Denver. JAMLAC exists to meet the legal needs of oppressed men and women living in poverty. It is a safe and confidential place for those who have nowhere else to turn. Pamela has chosen to use her education and profession to bring light to some very dark places—but she doesn't stop there.

She also loves theater and has a background in acting. Every year she coaches or acts on a local theatrical production. Her aim is to bring life, grace and humor to others through the art form she so dearly loves. She and her husband, Brad, have recently opened three rooms in their home to rent out. Every time I see her she tells me a new story about someone who stayed a few nights in her home. In almost all those stories Pamela or Brad were able to care well for a stranger.

And Pamela is honest with herself and others in such a healthy way. She holds her soul with humility, so much so that when people are around her they feel like they can be honest about who they are without fear of any judgment. Pamela understands her vocation so well, at times I wonder if she even knows how hard she works every day.

This is the kind of life and work we are invited to. And it's for all of us. It doesn't matter where we are employed. I did not have to leave my factory job to do God's work, and I do not have to work at or volunteer for a church to do God's work. As we continue to experience a changing faith, we will see God's work is done when we are simply willing to pay attention enough to find the sliver of light in the dark and tear it wide open.

By this point you may be wondering whether you are truly engaging with God in his work in this world. To answer this question we would do well to ask a few more questions: If someone were to follow you around for a week, what would they say you are really about? What are the things you care about? What do you spend most of your time paying attention to? How do you treat others? How do you view yourself?

How we respond to these questions may reveal what we believe about our work in this world.

One thing is for sure: God is here, and he is working in this world. He invites us to move from toil and toward joining him in his work.

10

From Nowhere to Everywhere

███

There was a time in my life when I tried to move past the idea of God, because I did not want to think about him or her—or whatever God might be. So I spent my time focused on others things and stopped paying attention to God. What I did not know was that even in those days God was still there. He always has been, is now and always will be. The question is whether we are willing to wake up to this. This is what King David was getting at when he wrote the words:

> Where can I go from your Spirit?
>> Where can I flee from your presence?
> If I go up to the heavens, you are there;
>> if I make my bed in the depths, you are there.
> If I rise on the wings of the dawn,
>> if I settle on the far side of the sea,
> even there your hand will guide me,
>> your right hand will hold me fast.
> If I say, "Surely the darkness will hide me
>> and the light become night around me,"
> even the darkness will not be dark to you;

> the night will shine like the day,
> for darkness is as light to you. (Psalm 139:7-12)

His poem teaches us there is not one place in all of existence where God is not present. God is in the holy places that cultivate an awareness of his presence. God is also in the dark places we'd rather not think about.

The prophet Isaiah spoke of this promise to King Ahaz in the midst of a hopeless situation. When Ahaz was king of Judah, the kings of Israel and Aram laid siege to Jerusalem, waiting to attack. In the midst of this political crisis God said to Ahaz, "Be careful, keep calm and don't be afraid. Do not lose heart" (Isaiah 7:4). But God did not stop there. He knows the human capacity for not trusting him, so he said to Ahaz, "Ask the LORD your God for a sign, whether in the deepest depths or in the highest heights" (Isaiah 7:11). Even still, Ahaz refused to acknowledge God.

God gave Ahaz a sign anyway. Isaiah told the king, "the LORD himself will give you a sign: The virgin will conceive and give birth to a son, and will call him Immanuel" (Isaiah 7:14). Immanuel means "God with us." In the midst of a looming war, certain death and political agreements, God made a promise to Ahaz: "I am with you."

Even still, King Ahaz ignored the promise. He believed Assyria was the one thing he could count on. He was outmatched, so he made a deal with the Assyrian king to come and rescue him. At first glance this is no big deal. King Ahaz's country had a weak military and needed the help of a global military superpower like Assyria. Ahaz possessed the necessary diplomatic skills to broker the deal. But, like any political situation, there is always more to the story.

Ahaz won the aid of Tiglath-Pileser III, Assyria's king, by writing him a psalm of praise. Ahaz paid tribute to this king, offered him money from gifts devoted to God and worshiped Tiglath-Pileser as a god. As a result, Assyria came to the aid of King Ahaz and delivered him from his enemy.

I can't say I blame him. There have been times in my life when things seem hopeless and impossible. I've tried everything to get out of a jam, to make life easier and to feel better about my situation. In those moments, everything inside me feels like saying, "God is with us? Really?"

Sometimes it's hard to believe God is anywhere. Whether it's the noise and distractions we've welcomed into our lives, the daily, unspeakable tragedies we read about in the news or the doubts deep inside about God's existence. Sometimes it feels like the best we can say is, "If God is with us, then where is he?"

> Sometimes it feels like the best we can say is, "If God is with us, then where is he?"

ARE YOU DEAF?

As much as the psalmists spoke of God being everywhere, they also had times when they shouted at God in complete exasperation. David wrote,

> My God, my God, why have you forsaken me?
>   Why are you so far from saving me,
>   so far from my cries of anguish?
> My God, I cry out by day, but you do not answer,
>   by night, but I find no rest. (Psalm 22:1-2)

These are the very words Jesus cried out as he hung on the cross. His experience was so dark in that moment; his own Father had abandoned him. Another psalmist wrote,

> Why, LORD, do you reject me
>   and hide your face from me? . . .

You have taken from me friend and neighbor—
   darkness is my closest friend. (Psalm 88:14, 18).

For thousands of years men and women have cried out to God, asking, Where are you? There are seasons when the idea of Immanuel seems to mock us, times when God may be somewhere, but certainly not where we are. Whether it's a natural disaster, a cheating spouse, another mass shooting, a terminal diagnosis or a loved one who passed away, life can press in so hard and deep we are left to ask, Where is God in all this? Some believe the answer is that God is *not* with us.

After the horrific events in Newtown, Connecticut, at Sandy Hook Elementary School, some suggested it was precisely because God was not there that this heinous act happened. They claim we should not be surprised to see this kind of violence since we have removed God from our schools.

This misguided belief assumes we somehow possess the power to remove God from certain places. When we think this way, we begin to look for God only in specific places. When we do this we are bound to miss him in many other places.

We cannot go anywhere God is not. We are constantly in the middle of the presence of God at all times and in all places. He is always on the move, speaking to us and reaching out to humanity. The sound of God is a constant "reverberation . . . caused by the motion of all things, which fills the whole world and which accompanies the human voice and every other sound."

Which brings me back to my wanting to move past the idea of God—this all happened a little more than ten years ago. My wife and I call this the period our "two years from hell." In less than two years we experienced eight out of the top ten causes of stress. The worst part of all this was being asked to leave the church I helped start. Those who my wife and I believed were our closest friends, those we trusted most, asked me to resign with no warning and no reason. We lost friends and relationships and felt alone. It felt like hell because it even seemed God was nowhere.

I was hurt, disillusioned and angry. I was certain I'd never be a pastor again and more certain the church and I were done. My relationship with God and belief in him hung by a thread. These were dark days. I knew life had gotten the better of me when I ended up in the hospital hooked up to a heart monitor because of chest pains. The doctor later told me, "Your heart is trying to figure out what 'normal' is, because your life has been chaos."

In the midst of my darkest days my friend Jim called me constantly. Jim was a pastor of a local church and had become a good friend. He never tried to convince me of anything. He just called to check in with me and remind me he loved me. His compassion wore me down, not in an exasperating way, but much like water slowly smoothing a ragged edge on a stone.

After several months of staying far away from the church, my wife and I decided to visit Jim's church one Sunday. We arrived a few minutes late and decided we would just slip in the back and sit down. Just as we walked through the doors in the back of the auditorium, the congregation sang the words:

Great is Thy faithfulness, O God my Father;
There is no shadow of turning with Thee;
Thou changest not, Thy compassions, they fail not;
As Thou hast been, Thou forever will be . . .

I slumped to my seat with my head in my hands, tears dripped from my eyes, and I heard God saying over and over, "You can give up on me, but I will never give up on you." He had been saying this to me forever, even in the midst of the pain, the wounds and the betrayal. But it took that moment for me to finally hear his words and become aware of his presence.

I shared this experience with a friend of mine, and he asked me where I thought God had been the whole time. I made some comment about him being far away and ignorant of my pain. When I finished talking he paused, looked me dead in the eye and said, "No, God was right there with you in the midst of it all."

> I heard God saying over and over, "You can give up on me, but I will never give up on you."

He led me through a prayer and invited me to return to the moment of my greatest pain over the last two years. I remembered it perfectly. It was an early morning in my kitchen. My wife and I had just experienced a total betrayal from some of our closest friends. We sat on our cold, white tile kitchen floor weeping. Our son, who was nearly two years old at the time, cried with us, not because he was struggling but because he wanted us to stop. It was the lowest point of my life.

As my friend prayed over me, I felt as if I was back in that kitchen again. I felt the cold kitchen tiles, saw the old white cabinets in our kitchen along with the outdated blue countertops. I heard the cries of my wife and son, and felt my warm tears on my cheeks. He then asked, "Where do you see Jesus?" And for the first time in my life I had eyes to see exactly where he was. He was sitting on the cold, white tiles of our kitchen floor with my wife, my son and me, and he was crying too.

God was right there, with us, in the pain and heartache of that moment. It's no wonder Jesus was called Immanuel. We see in the pain and suffering of Jesus a God who will not be kept out, One who says, "I know your pain, and I am in this with you." When I woke up to this, I experienced a change in my faith and was finally able to say "God is here."

While I experienced God's presence and his speaking through prayers and old hymns, it turns out he is not limited in how he speaks. My friend Marcus told me about the time God spoke to him through the rapper Eminem; he encountered God's love and grace in the place he least expected to find it.

Marcus works every day with a lot of broken people. Some days it is exciting and rewarding. There are many days when people experience breakthrough and healing, and take huge strides toward wholeness. Then there are other days when people relapse, the marriage doesn't work out or healing doesn't happen. When these dark days come, they seem to come all at once.

One stretch of particularly dark days, Marcus had enough. He felt hopeless and angry, and told God he didn't believe things would ever change for the better. He got home, turned on his stereo system, and played Eminem's album titled *Recovery*.

Now, there is something we should know about hip-hop albums. They are rarely meant to be a collection of random songs. Instead, each song is one small part of a larger narrative. If you really want to hear a hip-hop album, and not just listen to it, you need to play it all in one sitting. This is exactly what Marcus did.

The opening words of the album confirmed Marcus's attitude about things not getting better. Eminem raps about how things don't change. The lyrics are offensive to everyone. In his typical style, Eminem tells the world what they can do, where they can go and how they can get there. Then, in the middle of the song, Eminem is struck by lightning. He calls out to God for forgiveness, and God replies by forgiving his sins. Marcus thought Eminem had lost his edge and had gone soft.

Over the next few songs the lyrics spoke about hitting bottom, his self-hatred, his near-death experience from overdosing and how he is doing all he can to make his life and relationships right. The sixth track on the album is titled "Going Through Changes." Marcus told me by the time the song was finished he was in tears. He said, "It was like God was screaming at me, 'I want to change everyone and everything for the better!'"

Sometimes God speaks through prayers and old hymns; other times he speaks through Eminem. He is always present, always speaking everywhere; it's just a matter of whether we are willing to pay attention. For God, there are no sacred places and secular places. He is in both. The lines that we have created are constantly blurred by his presence.

> Sometimes God speaks through prayers and old hymns; other times he speaks through Eminem.

This is how God works. We can see his glory when standing atop a mountain soaking in indescribable beauty, or when sitting in a back alley looking into the eyes of a homeless man. We can hear his voice in words of love spoken from a friend, and in criticism directed at us from an enemy. We can find his words in a verse from Scripture or in a stanza of a poem.

It's just a matter of whether we are able or willing to see him. There are moments when it's harder to see God, but it's not just circumstances that make it hard to be aware of God's presence. Sometimes it is the way we choose to organize our lives.

A DIVIDED HEART

Many of us live very compartmentalized lives. Some places in our hearts are open, and we are okay talking about them. But then there are other places, spaces we don't like to go and certainly don't want God meddling in either. I know this all too well. I can compartmentalize parts of my life with the best of them.

I did not set out to live this way, but several years ago I woke up to see my divided heart. It turns out I stuff things. Much of my life people have told me how direct I am, how honest I am, and how I "tell it like it is." What they didn't know is for everything I said, there were many things that went unsaid. I would bury things, believing it was easier to deal with life this way.

I have since learned that burying something does not deal with anything. It just allows pain, bitterness, anxiety and wounds to grow their roots deeper in my soul. I wanted to think I could shut one part of my life down and operate smoothly in another, but it didn't work. I failed to see that I operate out of one heart. Whatever I bury in it will seep into all places of my life.

Something in us knows this, but we still attempt to live divided lives. We create all kinds of compartments so we can manage our lives well. And it's not always bad things, but normal everyday things. We have the career compartment, which involves our job, work, skills and professional development. Many of us aren't thrilled with this compartment, but it provides money to enjoy the other parts of our life.

Then there is the family compartment: parents and siblings, and, for some, spouses and children. And many of us have a crazy cousin or uncle who only surfaces at weddings. And we have the relationships compartment composed of the "it's complicated" relationships: a boyfriend or girlfriend, old friends, BFFs and new friends.

Some of us have the religion compartment. It features church, ritual, theology, prayer and God. Many of us manage to get to this compartment only on a Sunday here and there, if at all. We also go to it when life unravels and we really need God to come through.

The more compartments we create in our hearts, the more we close them off, the harder they are to open. In my experience it's easy to shut God out of these other compartments and demand he stays in the little compartment we give him. The more we do this, the harder it is to be aware of his presence. We do this not only in our hearts but also in the world we live in.

We create all kinds of contexts and categories in our world. We decide one place is sacred and another is secular. Jesus didn't seem to think this way. He never seemed wrapped up in the places he was not supposed to go. Jesus had the ability to see his Father's presence everywhere in this world. He was as much at home in the temple as he was at the home of a tax collector. There was not one place in the world he was not willing to go.

IT'S ALL MINE

Twenty-six miles north of the town where Jesus lived was a Roman city called Caesarea Philippi. There were so many shrines to the god Pan in the city that it was also called Paneas. Pan was traditionally connected to sex, promiscuity and lust. Pan worshipers often engaged in sexual acts as a way of worship—not just with other humans but with animals too. All of this was a way for them to satisfy their primal sexual urges.

What's worse is that Pan worshipers did not worship him behind the walls of a temple but in open-air grottos. Many of their rituals were done in the open, within view of everyone. It's safe to say this was not a place for the family.

Most anyone I know, including myself, would stay away from a place like this. If we were ever to draw lines and boundaries about places we would not go, Caesarea Philippi—Paneas—would no doubt top the list. But that's the thing about Jesus; he never seems to operate by our rules.

Matthew's Gospel tells about a time Jesus brought his disciples to Caesarea Philippi. There Jesus asked them who people believed he was. His disciples replied, "Some say John the Baptist; others say Elijah; and still others, Jeremiah or one of the prophets" (Matthew 16:14). After they answered, Jesus asked, "But what about you? . . . Who do you say I am?" Peter responded, "You are the Messiah, the Son of the living God" (Matthew 16:15-16).

Jesus blessed Peter for his answer, and said, "I tell you that you are Peter, and on this rock I will build my church, and the gates of Hades will not overcome it" (Matthew 16:18). The gates of Hades was not a figure of speech. In fact, it was a cave not far from the Grotto of Pan. Those who lived in the city believed the cave was the gateway to the underworld, where the gods came and went.

It is right in this place Jesus said all the powers of hell will not withstand the force of his kingdom here on this earth. Why? Because God's presence is everywhere, and not even the gates of hell can hold him back. This was a powerful moment for the disciples. Not just because Peter identified Jesus, but because of where they were.

Jesus' going to Paneas would have no doubt raised the eyebrows of many. But he didn't care about that. He cared about the people in those places, and he wanted his disciples to know if they were to be like him they had to be willing to go these places too. Anytime we create our own safe world, separate ourselves from others and draw dividing lines, we risk missing God's presence everywhere in this world.

The church often has built walls to keep others out instead of forging pathways so we can go out and all can come in. We don't have to look far to find a Christian leader decrying the evil of the world. But perhaps our world is so broken precisely because too many of us have refused to interact with it. If things are really as dark as we think, why do many choose not to enter the darkness with the light?

> The church often has built walls to keep others out instead of forging pathways so we can go out and all can come in.

Let's not forget God moves in the direction of brokenness, darkness, sin, suffering and pain. God never stands apart from humanity; he pursued us from the moment we chose to walk away from him. Why would we think we could live any different?

Jesus was pretty straightforward. He assumes that his followers will go anywhere and everywhere and serve everyone so as many as possible would hear of the hope he brings. Jesus wants us to be like him. It's not just inviting people to our parties but going to their parties too. It's not just opening our doors and inviting others in, but saying yes to the invitations of all people.

This is why, just before Jesus ascended back to heaven, he commanded his disciples to "go" (Matthew 28:19). He did not tell them, or us, to only invite people into our safe places, where we believe God already is. He *sent* his people into this good world he created— a world saturated with the presence of God.

I imagine when his disciples heard his command they did not wonder if any place was off limits. They were with Jesus at Paneas. They were also there when he ate with sinners and prostitutes and tax collectors. They knew the whole world was theirs. Those who follow Jesus can have the same confidence. We can go anywhere knowing God is there—even places like Paneas.

JESUS AT A PORN SHOW

Perhaps the closest things to Paneas in our world today are the many porn conventions that happen every year across the world. Years ago, in Grand Rapids, I had lunch with a fellow named Craig Gross. Craig and his friend Mike Foster knew that a porn convention was one place where many assumed God was absent. They thought differently.

They decided to go to the national porn convention in Las Vegas and set up a booth so people would know God is here. They handed out Bibles with "Jesus Loves Porn Stars" on the cover. This simple step gained national media attention and led to an organization that has helped countless people out of porn addiction and helped many leave the porn industry.

I asked Craig what made them think of doing that. His answer, as I recall, was quite simple. He wondered about places in our world where no one had gone with the good news of Jesus. It didn't take long to figure out it was the world of porn. So he went because Jesus said "go." He knew even in the darkest places, God was present. In doing so he has seen God's presence in unbelievable ways.

People like Craig know the heart of the psalmist who wrote, "The earth is the LORD's, and everything in it, the world, and all who live in it" (Psalm 24:1).

We seem to limit God's presence far more than he does. We seem to pay more attention to one place than others. Thus we miss the fact that the earth is dripping with God's presence, not just in some places but in all—even Paneas and porn conventions.

The prophets spoke of the day when all of humanity would wake up to God's presence. Habakkuk spoke of the day when "the earth will be filled with the knowledge of the glory of the LORD as the waters cover the sea" (Habakkuk 2:14). Isaiah had a vision and heard angels calling out, "Holy, holy, holy is the LORD Almighty; the whole earth is full of his glory" (Isaiah 6:3). The psalmist longs for us to wake up to this, writing, "may the whole earth be filled with his glory" (Psalm 72:19).

All of this points to the fact that God is with us here and now. We can live today as if it is tomorrow, when all people on earth will have eyes to see his glory. No more will there be the divisions of sacred and secular—we will finally have eyes to see it's all sacred, because our world is soaked in the presence of God himself.

This promise comes to us not just in the good times but in the bad times too, in the moments when we wonder if God is anywhere. It pries open the compartments we create and asks us to trust that God wants our whole heart. It floods into all places in our world, including the places we'd rather not go. When we are able to open ourselves up, we will experience a changing faith.

We are invited to open our eyes and see this now, to wake up to God's presence a little more each day. So one day we can stand together and proclaim the good news that indeed "God is here!"

11

From Bad News to Good News

■ ■ ■

The other day, while at a stoplight, an old Mercedes Benz station wagon covered in bumper stickers sat in front of me. There were political bumper stickers, comical bumper stickers and two Denver Broncos stickers. The one that caught my attention, however, said, "If Jesus Is the Answer, What Is the Question?"

It was intended to mock the old bumper stickers that said "Jesus Is the Answer," and it did its job well. But more than that, it provided a much-needed critique about the way we speak of Jesus.

I'm not sure I know anyone who walks around saying "Jesus is the answer." It's quite possible we believe Jesus *is* the answer, and yet may struggle with a response to the bumper sticker on that Mercedes Benz.

Many of us are willing, able and eager to speak about Jesus, but we often miss the starting point. While we believe the answer is Jesus, we're unaware of the questions people are asking. Chances are we give answers to questions no one is asking. And there is nothing more boring than an answer to a question that hasn't been asked.

This may be one of the greatest points of disconnection between the world and the church today. We are living in new times, which means there are new questions that demand new answers. Too often

we ignore today's questions and are content to respond with yesterday's answers. Is it any wonder so many have stopped listening?

I believe that Jesus' message, life, death, burial and resurrection
are good news, but we must first stop presuming we know the questions being asked in our world. We
first must listen to others and hear
the questions they ask. Only then
can we begin to help them make
sense of Jesus, the good news we
call the gospel and how it connects
to the questions people ask today.

> We are living in new times,
> which means there are
> new questions that
> demand new answers.

When I was a teenager I was constantly bombarded with messages others believed to be good news. I attended a Christian high
school, and every week we had to attend chapel with guest speakers.
One particular speaker was in his late fifties and was obviously pas-
sionate about teenagers. He was introduced by our principal,
bounded up to the stage, grabbed the microphone, raised his arm
in the air and greeted us with "What's up homies?"

Homies?

We were a homogenous, suburban, Christian high school in
West Michigan who were whiter than a gallon of milk. We never
used the term *homies*. Our student body figured out in no time he
had no idea who we were.

He went on to speak about how hard it was to be a teenager,
saying, "I know exactly what it's like to be where you are." I remember thinking, *No you don't.* This guy graduated from high
school more than two decades before I did. How could he possibly
think he knew what life was like for a high school kid in 1994?

This was not the only time I felt this way. Throughout my high
school years many wanted to talk *at* me about Jesus, but few
wanted to speak *with* me. I heard all kinds of answers, the
problem is none of them responded to the questions I had. As a

result, I stopped listening to most of what people had to say.

I not only grew tired of hearing answers that didn't matter; I had a deeper suspicion. If those who wanted so badly to help me wouldn't take the time to listen, I wondered if they cared about me at all. Looking back, I know I wasn't alone in feeling like this—not then and not now. When this happens, our normal response is to stop listening.

As we wrestle with our changing faith we must engage in meaningful ways with questions people are asking. It requires moving from speaking first to listening first. We

> If those who wanted so badly to help me wouldn't take the time to listen, I wondered if they cared about me at all.

may believe we have the good news of Jesus, but we must first know what the bad news is. Then we can respond to others in a way that matters.

THE UNKNOWN GOD

Luke, who is believed to have written the book of Acts, told a story about the time the apostle Paul visited the city of Athens. He arrived alone and spent some time observing the city. It didn't take long for Paul to notice the number of idols, temples and altars that littered the city.

Historians suggest there were more than three thousand altars in the central marketplace alone, where citizens offered gifts to the gods. They even had an altar to the "Unknown God," just to be safe. They could not be sure they knew of all the gods, so they sacrificed to the unknown god so he or she could accept their offerings as worship.

Paul saw how serious the Athenians were about religion. They were deeply devoted to their gods, participated in religious rituals and worshiped them. On seeing this Paul's heart was stirred, and he "reasoned in the synagogue with both Jews and God-fearing

Greeks, as well as in the marketplace day by day with those who happened to be there" (Acts 17:17).

Paul did not preach at them about how terrible their gods, altars and temples were. He didn't presume to know the culture or the people of Athens. He "reasoned," which means he took part in a dialogue. He not only spoke but also listened.

Eventually, Paul was invited to go to a meeting at the Areopagus or Mars Hill. Because it was the center for religious, political, educational and philosophical thought, an influential and powerful group met there. Some philosophers heard Paul, brought him to Mars Hill and said, "You are bringing some strange ideas to our ears, and we would like to know what they mean" (Acts 17:20).

Paul's reply to their question showed he understood their bad news: "People of Athens, I see that in every way you are very religious" (Acts 17:22). Paul affirmed them. He knew the Athenians took their worship seriously. They were devoted to their gods. Paul did not demonize them but showed respect for their culture and their religion. Paul told those present he "looked carefully" at their idols and altars (Acts 17:23). He observed before he judged.

There is an ancient piece of wisdom that says, "Give everybody the benefit of the doubt" (*Mishnah Avot* 1:6). Don't we wish others would do that for us? I've learned that when I first jump to judgment, I am typically wrong. Like many of us, I often presume to know more than I do about a person or an issue. No matter how often I am wrong, I struggle with rushing to judgment. At the same time, I get so frustrated when others judge me.

There have been many times when someone has judged me, made a comment about who they think I am or formed an opinion about my life before speaking to me. While it drives me absolutely crazy, I have to recognize I often am guilty of doing the same thing to others. I end up judging those who are judgmental. It's easy to point a finger at those who are pointing fingers. It's easy to yell back at those who yell at us. In the end, we prove we are just like them. Paul didn't do anything like this.

He observed the people and culture of Athens, and showed respect for who they were. Some credit Mother Theresa with saying when we judge people we

> It's easy to point a finger at those who are pointing fingers. In the end, we prove we are just like them.

have no time to love them. Paul chose love and spoke from that place. He did not judge; he simply observed the city, its citizens and their worship.

In his careful observations Paul had noticed the altar to an "Unknown God." In his Mars Hill address he said, "you are ignorant of the very thing you worship—and this is what I am going to proclaim to you" (Acts 17:23). He used the objects they were familiar with and spoke to their bad news with the good news of Jesus. He told them of the God who fashioned the world and everything we see. But he didn't stop there.

He told them this God does not live in temples like the gods of Athens, nor does he demand humans serve him. The "Unknown God" does not demand anything of us, rather he is the one who "gives everyone life and breath and everything else" (Acts 17:25).

The philosophers Paul addressed did not have categories for gods who freely gave gifts to humanity. Many of those gathered there believed the gods were hard to please, and the best one could hope for was to keep them happy *most* of the time—certainly not all the time. They believed the gods laid heavy demands on mortals, and if those demands were not met the gods grew angry.

This belief ran so deep the philosopher Apollonius, who was a contemporary of Paul, said, "it is a much greater proof of wisdom and sobriety to speak well of all the gods, especially at Athens, where altars are set up in honor even of unknown gods." Apollonius knew it was good to ensure the gods thought well of the people.

They were consumed with giving good things to the gods.

This is why Paul spoke first and foremost of the God who gives good things. He proclaimed a message of hope and love, which they, and we, desperately need. Paul proclaimed that God wasn't distant or removed. He is close enough to touch, and longs for a vibrant relationship with humanity.

Paul quoted their poets: "God did this so that they would seek him and perhaps reach out for him and find him, though he is not far from any one of us. 'For in him we live and move and have our being.' As some of your own poets have said, 'We are his offspring'" (Acts 17:27-28). Paul's message was drenched in hope and dripping with grace. He invited those listening to move from bad news toward the good news of Jesus.

THE GOOD NEWS IS STILL GOOD

In our world today there is no shortage of bad news. We are all too familiar with pain, suffering, disillusionment and brokenness. Every time we encounter this we have hundreds of questions. The hope Paul spoke of yesterday is still good news today, because Jesus is the same yesterday, today and tomorrow.

The story of Jesus tells us God did not sit up in some heavenly realm far away and wince at the pain and agony of humanity. Rather, in the person of Jesus he jumped with both feet into the mess we have made. Jesus took on our sorrow, anxiety, suffering, disappointment, sin and shame. People despised and rejected him. He was a man well acquainted with suffering, and was familiar with pain (Isaiah 53:3). He is not a God who needs anything but who gave up everything so we could experience freedom, know hope and receive grace.

I've often wondered why God didn't do a bit of magic, wave his hand and make everything on earth better. It would have saved him and us a lot of suffering. And therein lies the paradox of Jesus and the cross. By entering our pain and taking on our brokenness, he has provided hope and shown us healing.

When Jesus hung on that damnable cross, humanity witnessed the greatest suffering. For on Jesus hung the darkness, suffering, sin and shame of the world. But at this same moment humanity witnessed the greatest hope. For in the suffering of Jesus God tells us he is with us the midst of the mess, and that will never change.

This is why the good news does not invite us to run from or fight against our pain. Nor should we pretend everything is okay. The good news is not a Band-Aid for an otherwise broken life. The good news is better than that.

Every last word of the Bible screams, "You are not beyond hope. Not now. Not ever." It is not a message about avoiding an angry God, but one that invites us to meet the God who suffers with us. Because of this, in the midst of our brokenness we can know that it doesn't have to end this way.

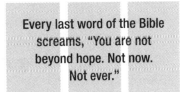

Every last word of the Bible screams, "You are not beyond hope. Not now. Not ever."

The good news does not end with suffering and death. When Jesus breathed his last and was buried, he took all our sin, shame and pain with him to the grave. Then came the resurrection. When Jesus came out of the grave, he left all the sin, shame and pain buried. In the midst of our bad news, we can still find hope, grace, love, compassion and forgiveness.

Perhaps God has done this so we would "seek him and perhaps reach out for him and find him." This message tells us even in our worst moments Jesus "is not far from any one of us" (Acts 17:27). This is the good news for our bad news. If we proclaim anything less than this, we have missed the point. And when we embrace this good news, we can enter the bad news of others to show them what Jesus looks like.

A HOSPITAL AND A MAILBOX

In India, the Dalits, also known as the "Untouchables," are lower than the bottom rung of society. They have a history of being oppressed, exploited, beaten, victimized, raped and forced into slavery. They are among the poorest people in the world.

My friend Mike has a pastor friend who lives, serves and works among the Dalits. This pastor recently spoke about a group who visited him to see his work among the Untouchables. The visitors' hearts were ripped out, and they were in utter shock at what they saw.

They witnessed children dying from dysentery and malnutrition; their bodies were often left on the streets or outside houses. Because Dalits are not seen as human beings in the eyes of many, including those in law enforcement, they are routinely forced out of the places they live. They have little recourse to address the situation. Many crimes committed against them are not investigated, because the government does not acknowledge their existence.

The distraught visitors knew they had to do something to address this gross injustice and oppression. They wasted no time. After they returned home, they put together a plan to bring much-needed aid, resources and help to this community. They decided to raise funds to build a hospital so they could provide medical help the Dalits so desperately needed.

While the funds were being raised on the other side of the world, the pastor who lived and worked among the Dalits met with the elders of the community. After listening to them about their daily troubles and their struggle to be seen as human, he asked, "What do you need? What is one thing I can do?"

The elders said in unison, "We need a mailbox."

The pastor thought to himself, *A mailbox? Really?* Confused, he said to them, "Why do you need a mailbox?"

The explained: if they were able to get a mailbox in their slum, they would then need a zip code. And if the government issued them a zip code it would be forced to recognize them as humans. As a result they would be granted rights and access to recourses that would bring healing to their community.

It seemed simple enough. The pastor would go through the proper channels, speak to the right authorities and get a mailbox. But this isn't what happened. The pastor and members of his church met strong resistance. The Dalits were hated, and anyone who helped them were hated just as much. So getting a mailbox proved to be a long, painful process.

In the meantime, the necessary funds were raised for the hospital. Construction began and after some time the hospital opened. However, no one from the Dalit community went to receive medical care from the hospital. They were content to wait for a zip code.

After two years of legal battles, being threatened and physical attacks, the pastor and his church got a mailbox. And when they got the mailbox, they got a zip code. The Dalit community would finally be seen as human beings.

They celebrated the victory together, and the pastor sat with the elders of the community. He finally said to them, "Have you ever wondered why we joined with you to get a mailbox?"

To his surprise the elders said, "No. We know why you joined with us."

"Really?" The pastor said a little surprised.

"Yes," they said, "we know you are a pastor who believes in Jesus. And we now know who he is because we have watched you and your people. We now believe in Jesus too."

They also told the pastor that while they appreciated those who built the hospital, they would not go there. Many in the community were afraid of those who built it because they never came and lived among the Dalit community. "We now do not need the hospital, because we have a mailbox," they explained.

That pastor knew the bad news of the Dalit community, not only because he heard them talk about it but also because he identified with them, allowed their problems to be his and shared in their pain. He discovered their bad news and recognized it was the ragged opening for the good news.

Sometimes the good news is not found in a hospital but in something as simple as a mailbox.

12

From Fear to Love

∎∎∎

'm not sure any of us are well acquainted with love. I say this
because we are a people consumed with fear. Fear resides deep
within us, and it's unbelievably subtle. I'm not talking about the
kind of fear we experience when
we are face to face with imminent
danger. This is the kind of fear I experienced just last week.

I'm not sure any of us are well
acquainted with love. I say this
because we are a people
consumed with fear.

My wife and I had some friends
at our house, and most everyone
stayed rather late. By the time the last person left it was just after
midnight. My wife went to bed, and I stayed downstairs washing
dishes and cleaning up the kitchen.

I stood at the sink and heard the sound of footsteps just outside
our home. I looked outside and our neighbor's motion light turned
on. I'd like to tell you I grabbed my cape and switched into superhero
mode, but that would be a lie. Instead I grabbed my phone, dialed
911 and was ready to push the send button to make the call.

Our neighborhood has its fair share of crime. It's not uncommon
to have police helicopter search lights shining in our back yard. With
this knowledge fully in my mind, I slowly walked into or living room,

looking out the back window. It was then I noticed our back door was unlocked. Just as I made this observation I heard more footsteps and our motion light right outside the door turned on. I was sure there was a person standing at our door, wearing a terrifying mask, brandishing a weapon and intent on doing me bodily harm.

I looked out our window, and to my relief there was no one there. So I moved closer to the window to get a good look outside. I drew close enough that my breath fogged it up a little. And suddenly a man jumped up in front of the window, turned and sprinted across our yard toward our back gate. I was so startled I jumped back, stumbled over the edge of our couch, let out a scream like a dog whose paw is stepped on, and nearly dropped my phone.

I quickly jumped up and looked back outside. That's when I noticed the guy was carrying two empty milk jugs. It turned out to be our milkman delivering our milk in the middle of the night. It took me more than five minutes to compose myself and resume normal breathing. My wife came downstairs to ask what happened. When I told her, she laughed and said, "I forgot to mention the milkman changed his delivery time." I could have used this news yesterday.

While that kind of sudden rush of adrenaline and fear is real and rather intense, it is not the kind of fear most of us live with day-to-day. The fear we carry inside us plays at a much lower volume, but it still carries immense influence in how we think, live and function. I carried this fear with me for years. It was a deep and abiding fear I had of God himself.

The first god I was introduced to was one who was ready to kill me and cast me into the lake of fire to burn forever. The way I heard others speak about him caused me to think he would even enjoy the whole process a little bit. As awful as this sounded, I was told I could avoid this horrendous punishment if I repented. It was not so much a message of hope but how I could avoid a great threat.

Know what I did? I repented. In fact, I repented multiple times every week just to ensure one of my "repentings" worked. No matter how much I tried, I could never get over the looming threat. Deep inside I wondered, *If God was willing to watch me fry forever before I believed in Jesus, what's to stop him from changing his mind if I don't do all I am supposed to do?* My religious devotion was rooted in fear, which is why it took me a long time to believe in the God of love.

NO NEED TO FEAR

Many of us struggle because we are not well versed in love. Even though "God is love" (1 John 4:8), we do not seem to understand who he is, because we are conditioned by fear. Perhaps this is why the command most frequently found in the Bible is "Do not be afraid."

Some claim it is found 365 times, in various forms, in the Bible. From Genesis to Revelation it seems to be on every page. God reminded his people over and over again. "Fear not!" "Do not be frightened!" "Be not afraid."

Beyond the command not to fear the psalmist wrote,

The LORD is my light and my salvation
  whom shall I fear?
The LORD is the stronghold of my life—
  of whom shall I be afraid? (Psalm 27:1)

And in another place:

The LORD is with me;
I will not be afraid. (Psalm 118:6)

We may wonder why; of all the things God commanded in the Bible, the command not to fear is one of the most frequent. Perhaps because every human being has to deal with fear every day. It's almost always been this way.

I say *almost* always because there was a time when there was no fear. The writer of Genesis speaks of a time when the first man and the first woman did not feel fear whatsoever. They were completely at home in their world and comfortable in their own skin. But then, fear came to them.

In Genesis 3 the man and the woman were tempted to abandon God's instruction and go their own way. And they did. They were instructed not to eat from one tree in the garden. But they just couldn't stay away from it. The woman ate the fruit and gave it to the man who was with her.

They saw they were naked and sewed fig leaves together as a covering. In that moment everything changed for the man and the woman—and for all of us. But the same cannot be said for the unchanging God. He was love before they ate the fruit, he was love after, he is still love today, and he will be love tomorrow.

What changed for the man and the woman, however, is they moved from love to fear. As they covered themselves up with fig leaves, they heard the sound of God's footsteps and hid in the trees of the garden. God called out to them and asked, "Where are you?" The man replied, "I heard you in the garden, and I was afraid" (Genesis 3:9-10).

The first words spoken after the humans sinned were about fear. This story is not just about them; it's also about us. Fear always accompanies sin. And it's safe to say we have all sinned, therefore we all experience fear. Fear is so normal we barely notice it anymore.

A few weeks ago I was sitting with a good friend who was physically abused as a child. He was going through a difficult stretch, and at one point in our conversation he said, "As far as I've come, and as much as I've healed from what happened to me, there are still times when all I can hear is the voice of fear. It's so controlling."

The day after spending time with him, a woman in our church shared how she never realized how much fear was "cultivated in her home." She said, "I grew up with it. It was normal, and I learned to see myself and my world through the lens of fear." Listening to them, I found myself feeling the same things.

My fear centers on failure. For much of my life, it felt like the one thing people could count on was my screwing up *again*. Every time I did, words like, "Well, there you go again. It's always you, isn't it?" were directed to me. It didn't take long for me to see myself as someone who could never get things right. I believed (and still do at times) my role in life was to disappoint people. This fear creeps up in me as a husband, father, pastor, author and friend.

This fear we feel inside is called shame. It's the belief that if anyone were to know the "real me," they would stop loving me, reject me and want nothing to do with me. It's the belief we are not enough, we never have been, and we never will be. As one friend said to me, "Shame is like a bulky backpack I can never seem to take off." Shame is fear. It's everywhere, and what's worse, our fears are exploited every day in our world.

Take a casual glance at our media. From the news to advertising to television, we are a dumping ground for fear. Not only is most of our news bad news. It's bad news that is going to make our lives a living hell. And is advertising any better? So much consumption is rooted in fear. And what about politics? Mark Danner observed fear is "political gold."

The political right and left make all kinds of claims as to why we should be afraid. Our political leaders craft messages about the opposing party that are rooted in fear. Our government identifies a group of people and tells the public they are a threat to our way of life. It's no surprise. One good way to build solidarity is to create fear in a group of people.

I wish I could say religion has been untouched by this pattern, but I'd be lying. Richard Rohr observes, "Religious history is a history of human sacrifice, animal sacrifice and many disguised attempts at self-flagellation. It's not a love affair, but usually a cautious standoff accompanied by ritual attempts to placate a distant and demanding God. This is so embedded into the human hardwiring now that it is very hard to eradicate."

In many ways, religion is an incubator for fear and shame. This is what I saw and experienced so many times. It scared all of us.

Religion is an incubator for fear and shame.

When I was in college, a few students were out drinking one night, and two of them were caught by the school's leadership. Both of them admitted they had a few drinks and were immediately expelled from the school. No questions, no attempt to understand— just expulsion.

Students around campus gossiped about them, and many students told those who were expelled they were awful for breaking the rules. One of the students was dating a girl who was told she should break up with him because of how wayward he was.

It's no surprise students did not rush to confess their sins at my college. Just the opposite. We hid them more, because we learned that it didn't work. Not long after these students were expelled I was caught drinking by the leadership of my school. And the fears I had about being expelled, ridiculed and judged were all realized. I was dismissed from the school. In no time the rumors about me abounded, and many students and faculty freely made known to one and all their opinions of me and my behavior.

My college wasn't the only place like this. I've experienced this at churches, ministries, high schools and many other places that identify as Christian. We are subtly taught in cultures like this to keep our mouths shut and not talk about the things we've done, because if we are caught, it's all judgment and rejection.

The problem is, stuffing these things inside forces many to feel like hypocrites and horrible people, which then produces intense feelings of guilt. Which is exactly why I say religion is an incubator for shame. According to Brené Brown, three things are needed for fear and shame to grow: silence, secrecy and guilt.

Too often religion has caused such intense feelings of fear that we reject being honest about how we have failed, because we've seen how people get beat up when they finally do. And who wants to go through that?

Many religious people are angry about so many things in our world today. One does not have to do or say much to raise the ire of the religious. Simply make a statement challenging someone's theological beliefs and get ready to reap the whirlwind. There is no shortage of toxic vitriol. Make a comment for or against a social issue, and the picket signs are raised before you even finish speaking. But this should be no surprise. It's been said anger is fear coming out.

Yesterday I was driving and had the car radio on scan. Station after station came and went. I finally stopped to listen to a preacher on the radio—one of my guilty pleasures.

The preacher yelled about how our country is moving in the wrong direction and is headed toward destruction. He decried our immorality, the evils of our media and our wicked government. He predicted doom and gloom, and called Christian men and women to rise up and take our nation back for God. It was classic fear mongering that is often preached from American pulpits.

I've heard preachers warn the government will go after churches who do not toe the party line. Some have claimed many in our country are out to destroy the Christian faith. When we are terrified by the prospect of our nation falling, chances are we have placed our hope in our government, national economy and military. Indeed, we are more acquainted with the voice of fear than we are the voice of love.

Still, this kind of talk stirs people up deep inside and causes great fear among the masses. While the response may seem good at first, what we forget is "people motivated by fear do not act well." As scary as all this may seem, there is no need to fear at all—even if all these doomsday prophecies happen. Because the church is at its best in the places where it is oppressed and persecuted.

If we disagree politically, fine, but we need not fear anything. Our king is alive and well. And should all the predictions of doom actually happen to us, we should stand back, for the church in America just might be at its best.

The irony is we live such fearful lives while worshiping the very God who says to us over and over, "Do not be afraid!" Perhaps if we reconsider who God is, we will see there is no reason to fear at all. We could stand with the psalmist and say, "Whom then shall I fear?" We would hear his invitation to move from fear to love.

While silence, secrecy and guilt serve as fertilizer for fear and shame, the weed killer for fear is empathy and light. And this is exactly what Jesus did through his life, death, burial and resurrection.

THE DEFEAT OF FEAR

Through Jesus we learn of a God who would not be kept from his people. He took on our suffering, pain, fear, pain, sin and brokenness. The empathy of Jesus is seen in his willingness to bear our sin and shame. Empathy is the ability to understand the pain, sorrow and shame of others to the extent that they become yours. It means to feel *with* others.

Jesus allowed our suffering to be is his suffering, and he exposed our pain when he was nailed to the cross. When Jesus was crucified he not only suffered with us, but exposed the shame, fear and guilt we carry deeply within us. In the moment of his greatest agony, our fear was brought to light. This is how fear was destroyed. In Jesus, the God who is love destroyed fear once and for all.

This is why Paul said, "God has not given us a spirit of fear, but of power and love and of a sound mind" (2 Timothy 1:7 NKJV). Paul knows that the love God is far greater than fear. Love and fear are not good dance partners. They cannot coexist.

John wrote, "perfect love drives out fear" (1 John 4:18). Fear cannot be where love is present. John knew if we hear the voice of fear it is not the voice of God. God's voice is love. This is why the psalmists could say with full confidence, "Whom then shall I fear?"

What would it be like to live outside of fear, shame, anxiety, stress and worry? How would our lives look different if we were not ashamed of who we are in all our glory and brokenness? What if the good news for all people is that we have nothing to be afraid of? What would our world look like if we were not afraid of one another anymore? How would this kind of thinking lead us toward a changing faith?

It's almost difficult to imagine, because we are conditioned to listen to the voices telling us we are not good enough, we are beyond help, or we cannot be forgiven. Not

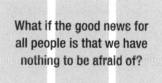

What if the good news for all people is that we have nothing to be afraid of?

only is this fear tangible and real, it is made worse by the media, politics and religion, which cultivate more fear in our hearts.

But the good news is love is greater than fear, which means we do not need to be afraid.

This is the message the angels spoke on the night Jesus was born. They said to the shepherds, "Do not be afraid. I bring you good news that will cause great joy for all the people" (Luke 2:10). This message is for "all the people" because all of us all struggle with fear. This has been the case since the garden, but it does not have to be this way.

No matter where we are in this moment. No matter how scared we might be. No matter how much shame we may carry. The good news says "Do not be afraid." We are invited into a changing faith by being open to the unchanging God who is love. God invites us to leave fear behind and become well-acquainted with love.

> We are invited into a changing faith by being open to the unchanging God who is love.

13

From Small Stories to a Big Story

∎∎∎

A **few years ago my wife** bought tickets for my birthday to see the Killers at Red Rocks Amphitheatre. Red Rocks is just ten miles west of Denver, settled between massive rock formations, with stunning views. I am not sure there is a better concert venue in the world. Then she told me we were going to the concert with our friends Dave and Kay, and I was so excited I could hardly contain myself.

The night of the concert came and the four of us went to dinner before we drove to Red Rocks. We found our way to our seats. The opening act came and went, and then we sat and waited. There were sound checks, guitar tuning, putting up the drum set, lights blinking here and there, and a host of other things being done in preparation for the show.

Then everything went black, and the crowd erupted. A few chords sounded and then Brandon Flowers burst on to the stage and began to sing. The Killers played for nearly two hours as the crowd sang along, danced and cheered at the end of every song. It was an amazing show in one of the greatest concert venues in the world.

Looking back, what I find interesting about the concert is how it was held together for two hours. Not any one person made the concert work, but everyone did a little. The musicians, sound engineers, roadies and lighting techs all played a part in the larger experience. Songs began and ended, none of which were connected to one another.

The songs did not employ the same tune or rhythm, had different lyrics and different time signatures. It was one concert with a ton of parts, but somehow it all held together and was seamless. Not only that, it provided a point of connection for everyone there. All those divergent, seemingly disconnected parts came together and gave us the experience of being connected to something bigger.

This is how I am learning to see the expansive story unfolding in our world. There are billions of people, families, beliefs, stories, experiences and cultures in our ever-changing world. And in the midst of it all there is one unchanging God knitting together a massive story, far bigger than any one place or time or person. He put all the divergent, seemingly disconnected parts together and invites us to experience being connected to something bigger. Because every story is bigger than any one person, it always involves other people, places and cultures.

BIGGER THAN YOU, BIGGER THAN ME

Our stories are always connected to others. I found myself connected to a story most unexpectedly when my son and I watched *Finding Nemo* for the first time. We made some popcorn, filled our cups with soda, sat on the couch and pushed play on the DVD player. By the end of film I was fighting back tears. My son looked at me, sat up, put his hands on my cheeks and said in the kindest, most concerned voice, "What's wrong, Daddy?" Yes, you can say I cried watching *Finding Nemo*.

It's not just that I am sentimental; it has to do with how and why

I found myself connected to the story being told. It involves an important part of my life, namely, my relationship with my father.

My dad and I often butted heads (which is putting it mildly). The older I got, the harder it became for us to live in peace. Though moments of goodness were scattered here and there, tension was the norm. Arguments, words spoken with intent to wound the other, fights, and screaming and yelling were a frequent part of our relationship. Over the years, layers of pain, hurt and unkind words built up. It was an endless cycle until the day things exploded. Deeply hurtful things were said, and as with any explosion, shrapnel shredded our hearts, causing more pain and hurt than ever. When the dust finally settled, we discovered nothing was left in its right place.

This resulted in my father and I not speaking to one another for nearly three years. I was a mixed bag of resentment, anger, remorse, bitterness and regret. I wanted nothing to do with him. My heart was bleeding and raw, and I knew I needed to do something so it did not end up destroying me.

During our time of noncommunication I decided to work toward healing, forgiving and grieving all that happened. Things got worse for me before they got better. For a time my feelings went beyond hating him; I was indifferent toward him. During this time I said to a friend, "If my dad died, I'm not sure I'd miss him. I think all I'd lose is the nostalgia of having a father who is still alive." I became angrier and more depressed as time went on. These were dark days. I struggled to get out of bed or to laugh with others. I even had a hard time enjoying my wife and children. But then, after nearly a year, something happened.

I prayed for my dad for the first time. I'm not sure how deeply I meant it, but I did it. What was really miraculous was the fact that I prayed for him. And I continued to do so. Some days I meant it more than others, but I willed myself to do it. As my cold heart thawed, I discovered how much I loved my dad. It was nothing new; I always had loved him, which is why the hurt and pain ran so deep.

What I did not know was that while I pursued healing and wholeness, my father also spent time working on his heart and soul. Neither of us spent our time blaming the other or stewing on how we hurt each another. We finally looked at ourselves and how we had been the cause of so much pain in our relationship. Years after not speaking to one another, we finally reconnected.

The first time we spoke was awkward, and I wasn't sure what to say. It felt like talking to someone you've just met. Looking back, it felt this way because, in more ways than I could count, we were both new people.

Several months after our first awkward conversation we sat together over a meal. I was overcome with how much he and I had gone through together. We had screamed, yelled and slugged it out over the years. But there we were, sitting, speaking with one another and sharing a meal. We had never known such peace. More than that, I no longer regretted our story and all we had gone through.

It is precisely our past, as ugly as some of it has been, that brought us to that table, and it was beautiful. Perhaps there were other, even better ways of getting there. But none of that mattered. What mattered is we sat together carrying the scars and memories of our difficult relationship, but those scars now meant something different.

They no longer spoke of pain and wounds and hurt. They now bore witness to God's love, grace and mercy. Sitting together was a tangible sign for me that love will always conquer conflict, that joy can heal despair and that God brings beauty from ashes. Today, I love the story of my dad and me because our relationship is no longer broken. It's now a story of healing.

Today we look ahead with great hope. We enjoy an amazing relationship and plan to continue building on it with the years we have left together as father and son. As we see it, there is no room for regret, only room for us to celebrate the fact that God has rebuilt, restored and renewed the relationship between us.

As important and meaningful as our story is, it's not just about Dad or me. It also involves my mom, who often felt torn between her husband and son. Our story also involves my wife, who walked with me as I addressed the pain of my relationship to my father. Our story now involves my children. As a dad, I want to do better, which is the same thing my father wants for me. Few things have played so large in my story as my relationship with my father and my relationship as a father.

Now, back to *Finding Nemo*, which is not the only movie that has brought me to tears. Several years ago I went to the theater with some friends to watch the film *Tree of Life* by Terrence Malick. After the film, I decided to go home even though my friends were going out. My friend Brian, who knows well the story of my relationship with my father, texted me a few hours later and asked, "How are you doing? I can imagine that film got under the hood for you." He was right. I found myself in the story *Tree of Life* told about a father and his sons.

It was the same thing with films like *Big Fish*, *Legends of the Fall*, *In America* and *Life Is Beautiful*. These stories speak about the beauty, love and struggle in relationships between fathers and sons. And this is exactly what good stories do. They do not merely present information, they invite us to interact and participate with them. Our experiences provide points of connection; they open something inside us we might otherwise miss.

> Good stories do not merely present information, they invite us to interact and participate with them.

Stories connect us to others, remind us we are not alone and tell us we are a part of something bigger than ourselves. This is something humans have always known. No story is ever about one person in one place in one culture—it's bigger than all of that. This is why we find stories so irresistible and powerful. That has never changed.

When we meet someone, this is why we want to know his or her story. We rarely ask for mere facts. Just this afternoon I sat with a couple I had just met. We told stories about our parents, our families and how we ended up in Denver. We learned we knew some of the same people, and subsequently told stories about them.

The longer we talked, the more points of connection we found. We tell our stories to others not just to be heard or known, but so others can find connections to their story and vice versa. We move from our small stories toward bigger stories. We long for these shared experiences, because deep inside we want to believe we are a part of something bigger than us.

> Stories connect us to others, remind us we are not alone and tell us we are a part of something bigger than ourselves.

And when we discover a story bigger than ours, we find we many points of connections with all kinds of different people. Jay-Z in his book *Decoded* wrote, "This is why the hustler's story—through hip hop—has connected with a global audience. The deeper we get into the sidewalk cracks and into the mind of the young hustler trying to find his fortune there, the closer we get to the ultimate human story, the story of struggle, which is what defines us all."

Humans have always told larger-than-life stories. We have developed stories, myths and legends that entire cultures identify with. These stories connect us. They are the glue that holds us together and give us a framework for understanding and meaning. These stories unite us because they provide a common point of connection that's bigger than movies, our culture or even with the human story.

Our stories ultimately provide a connection to the unchanging God who is the author of our stories. Because even as our stories change, there is a God who does not change, authoring a bigger story.

A STORY THAT DOESN'T CHANGE AT ALL

God embraces our divergent stories in all their agony and glory, and pieces them together. God uses every experience we have, both good and bad, to tell his unchanging story. He doesn't waste anything. Even our worst moments, the ones we wish had never happened, he will redeem. C. S. Lewis wrote, "That is what mortals misunderstand. They say of some temporal suffering, 'No future bliss can make up for it,' not knowing that Heaven, once attained, will work backwards and turn even that agony into a glory."

> God uses every experience we have, both good and bad, to tell his unchanging story. He doesn't waste anything.

This means our stories are an important part of the larger whole, and what we choose to do matters both now and forever. This is how God is telling his story, through everyday people like you and me. No matter how much our world changes or we change, the big story does not. There is great freedom in that.

We are free to hold on to all parts of our story, even those we'd like to forget. For years I wanted to forget about the story about my dad and me. It was a dark cloud that seemed to loom over my relationships with others, including my children, and especially with God. I had so much trouble with the idea of God as Father because I could not remove the image of my dad from the image of God.

It's no wonder I struggled to be honest with God, why I was scared of him, why I couldn't say I loved him, and why I always kept a comfortable distance from him. I didn't believe the promises that God was loving, compassionate and merciful. My relationship with Dad created a distorted connection to God.

Today, however, my healed relationship with Dad has created a deep trust and connection to God. I now know God turns our agony into glory. Because of the story God has written in my life and in the life of my dad, I can speak in ways I never could before of God's love and grace, and his ability to heal. This is a story of how God has taken a distorted connection to himself and created true love for him in my heart.

This is what God can and wants to do for all of us—no matter what story has unfolded in our lives. He is the unchanging God who will change and redeem our stories as a part of his larger story. This gives us confidence as we move from one place to a much better place. He's here, he's with us, he's on the move, and he invites us to move with him.

While yesterday, today and tomorrow may change, we serve a God who does not. Even though our world and our stories change, there is an unchanging God telling a cosmic story of redemption, renewal and restoration that does not change, and he invites us into a changing faith.

Acknowledgments

∎∎∎

Much love and many thanks to these incredible people:

Dave Neuhausel and Jon Gettings for their love and grace as I hunkered down and wrote this book during the long, cold winter months. I'm back.

Rachel Tyrrell for giving this book a "once over" and keeping my life sane. You're the best pastor wrangler out there.

Mike McFadden, Pamela VanderPool, Steve Beren, Amanda Pennington, Drew Bone, Dave Genova and Joe Leigh for walking with me, challenging me, encouraging me, holding my feet to the fire to stay healthy; for reading this book and offering strong critique and graceful insight. Thrilled to work alongside you.

My close community of brothers and sisters who constantly remind me "no man is a failure who has friends."

Cindy Bunch, Adrianna Wright, Deborah Gonzalez, Karli Saner, Drew Blankman and the team at IVP for their support, friendship and their tireless work on this book and on my behalf.

Greg Johnson for insisting there was a second book in there somewhere.

The Denver Community Church family for having the courage to take leaps, ask difficult questions, express real doubt and showing me how healthy faith really does change.

Beth, all these years later, and I am still lost for words—I hope I never find them.

Notes

■■■

CHAPTER 2: FROM CERTAINTY TO PROBABILITY

p. 31   more than forty thousand denominations in the world: "Status of Global Mission, 2014, in the Context of AD 1800–2025," Gordon Conwell Theological Seminary, accessed October 15, 2014, www.gordonconwell.edu/resources/documents/Status OfGlobalMission.pdf.

p. 32   "Americans are losing that place of meeting": Maya Angelou, "Maya Angelou's Cooking Advice: Ignore The Rules," *NPR*, December 16, 2010, www.npr.org/2010/12/16/132080094 /maya-angelous-cooking-advice-ignore-the-rules.

p. 35   "light is the splendor of the divine presence": Nahum M. Sarna, *Genesis*, JPS Torah Commentary (New York: Jewish Publication Society, 2001), p. 7.

CHAPTER 3: FROM DEFINITION TO DESCRIPTION

p. 42   "we have replaced idols with ideas": Peter Rollins, *How (Not) To Speak of God* (Brewster, MA: Paraclete, 2006), p. 10.

CHAPTER 4: FROM WORDS TO EXPERIENCE

p. 51   "Ann Voskamp wrote about her friend who often mails books": Ann Voskamp, "Dear Kids: What You Need to Know About Duck Dynasty, Justine Sacco, and Christmas," December 21, 2013, *A Holy Experience* (blog), www.aholyexperience.com /2013/12/dear-kids-never-forget-the-power-of-words-what -you-need-to-know-about-duck-dynasty-justine-sacco-and -christmas-2.

p. 53   "Words create worlds": Susannah Heschel, "Abraham Joshua
           Heschel," accessed October 9, 2014, http://home.versatel.nl
           /heschel/Susannah.htm.
p. 55   We use them to understand our world: Edward T. Hall,
           Beyond Culture (New York: Anchor Books 1976).

CHAPTER 5: FROM KNOWING TO UNKNOWING

p. 62   Comedian Pete Holmes on our ability to know anything:
           Pete Holmes, "Conan," TBS, March 21, 2011, www.youtube
           .com/watch?v=4LZPpP6HM6o.
p. 62   "When we know much about something": David McRaney,
           You Are Not So Smart (New York: Gotham, 2011), p. 79.
p. 65   we enter a process of doubt: Jack Mezirow, *Transformative
           Dimensions of Adult Learning* (San Francisco: Jossey-Bass,
           1991), p. 177.
p. 72   "unknowing becomes another kind of knowing": Richard Rohr,
           Falling Upward (San Francisco: Jossey-Bass, 2011), p. 112.

CHAPTER 6: FROM BEING RIGHT TO BEING FAITHFUL

p. 79   "an endless stretch of static, inky, black stillness": Brian Greene,
           "Is Our Universe the Only Universe?" *TED*, February 2012,
           www.ted.com/talks/brian_greene_why_is_our_universe
           _fine_tuned_for_life?language=en.

CHAPTER 7: FROM POWER TO TRUTH

p. 94   they are the last people we would think: Miroslav Volf, *God's
           Life in Trinity* (Minneapolis: Fortress, 2009), p. 127.
p. 96   Aristides's report to the Roman emperor: Aristides, *The
           Apology of Aristides* 15, www.newadvent.org/fathers/1012
           .htm.
p. 97   Marietta Jaeger Lane's story: "Forgiving Her Daughter's
           Murderer," ABC News, January 6, 2006, http://abcnews
           .go.com/2020/story?id=124051.

CHAPTER 8: FROM LEGALISM TO WHOLENESS

p. 107 Looking inside must always come first: Richard J. Foster, *Prayer* (New York: HarperOne, 2012), p. 24.

p. 108 trees were connected to primitive religious practices: Nahum M. Sarna, *Genesis*, JPS Torah Commentary (New York: Jewish Publication Society, 2001), p. 91.

CHAPTER 9: FROM TOIL TO WORK

p. 118 Like machines, humans became dispensable parts: Jacques Ellul, *The Technological Society* (New York: Vintage Books, 1967), p. 399.

p. 119 "toil is the misery of man": Abraham Joshua Heschel, *The Sabbath* (Farrar, Straus & Giroux, 2005), p. 16.

p. 119 wish we had spent more time working: Harold Kushner, *When All You've Ever Wanted Isn't Enough* (New York: Touchstone, 2002), p. 161.

p. 119 "the place where your deep gladness": Frederick Buechner, *Wishful Thinking: A Seeker's ABC*, rev. ed. (San Francisco: HarperOne, 1993), p. 119.

p. 123 "My position is that I write songs": Bono, "U2 Quotes," *Angelfire*, www.angelfire.com/mo/u2macphisto/U2quotespage.html.

CHAPTER 10: FROM NOWHERE TO EVERYWHERE

p. 130 The sound of God is a constant "reverberation": "Bat Kol," *The Jewish Encyclopedia* (New York: Funk & Wagnall's, 1906), 2:588, www.jewishencyclopedia.com/articles/2651-bat-kol.

CHAPTER 11: FROM BAD NEWS TO GOOD NEWS

p. 141 an answer to a question that hasn't been asked: Peter Kreeft, *Three Philosophies of Life* (San Francisco: Ignatius Press, 1990), p. 53.

p. 145 Apollonius on speaking well of the gods: Philostratus, *The Life of Apollonius of Tyana*, bk. 6, chap. 3.

CHAPTER 12: FROM FEAR TO LOVE

p. 155   fear is "political gold": Mark Danner, "The Politics of Fear,"
                New York Review of Books, November 22, 2012.

p. 155   Richard Rohr on fear: Richard Rohr, "Epiphany: You Can't Go
                Home Again," *St. Anthony Messenger*, accessed November 24,
                2014, www.americancatholic.org/messenger/jan2001/feature3
                .asp.

p. 157   Brené Brown on fear: Brené Brown, "Listening to Shame," *TED*,
                March 2012, www.ted.com/talks/brene_brown_listening_to
                _shame?language=en.

p. 158   "people motivated by fear do not act well": Mark Kurlansky,
                Nonviolence (New York: Modern Library, 2008), p. 184.

CHAPTER 13: FROM SMALL STORIES TO A BIG STORY

p. 166   Jay-Z on the hustler's story: Jay-Z, *Decoded* (New York:
                Spiegel & Grau, 2011), p. 172.

p. 166   They are the glue that holds us together: Jonah Sachs,
                Winning the Story Wars (Boston: Harvard Business Review
                Press, 2012), p. 92.

p. 167   "That is what mortals misunderstand": C. S. Lewis, *The Great
                Divorce* (New York: HarperCollins, 1963), p. 69.

Further Reading

∎∎∎

If you are interested in learning more about

The ever-changing church in our ever-changing world:
Tickle, Phyllis. *The Great Emergence.* Grand Rapids: Baker, 2008.

Our unpredictable world:
Greene, Brian. *The Fabric of the Cosmos: Space, Time, and the Texture of Reality.* New York: Random House, 2005.

Vocation:
Palmer, Parker J. *Let Your Life Speak: Listening for the Voice of Vocation.* San Francisco: Jossey-Bass; 1999.

Knowing how much we don't know:
Rohr, Richard. *Falling Upward: A Spirituality for the Two Halves of Life.* San Francisco Jossey-Bass; 2011.

Moving beyond defining God:
Rollins, Peter. *How (Not) to Speak of God.* Brewster, MA: Paraclete Press, 2006.

Finding words to speak to God:
Foster, Richard J. *Prayer: Finding the Heart's True Home.* San Francisco: HarperOne, 2002.

Living and telling bigger stories:
Sachs, Jonah. *Winning the Story Wars: Why Those Who Tell—and Live— the Best Stories Will Rule the Future.* Boston: Harvard Business Review Press, 2012.

Discussion Guide

∎∎∎

The following questions are offered as starting points for greater conversation about our changing faith. There isn't one right answer to any of these questions. They are intentionally open-ended so you can work through them together. You can use this guide with a friend, your book club, small group or family.

INTRODUCTION: GOING THROUGH CHANGES

1. "Jesus is the same yesterday, today and tomorrow. However, yesterday, today and tomorrow are not the same at all" (p. 11).

   What is your first response to this statement? Does this mean we have to reorient our faith? Should we throw away the faith from yesterday or keep some of it? What about tomorrow—can we have confidence in it?

2. "Change is the process of moving from somewhere to somewhere else" (p. 12).

   What changes do you observe in our world?

3. "Many of us held to certain beliefs about God, life, faith, church, religion and spirituality as though our lives and faith depended on it, but we cannot hold on to those anymore. We've let go of them, knowing we won't pick them up again.

   "What's more pressing, however, is the question, What beliefs will we pick up?" (p. 12).

We all have questions and doubts about God, life, faith, spirituality and religion. What are some of yours? What are the things you struggle to believe? What causes you to doubt? What gives you great hope? Where do you feel confidence? Write these things down, and if you are comfortable, share them with your discussion group.

CHAPTER 1: FROM CLOSED TO OPEN

1. "The more I learned, the more doubt crept into my life. If these people believed in the same God as the people in New York, then why were there so many lenses? How could it be that Christians could believe so many different things about God, life, faith, church, religion and spirituality?" (p. 19).

   When it comes to the Christian faith, there are many different, competing and even contradictory beliefs. How do we reconcile this? Is this positive? Negative? Why?

2. "Drew saw there are millions of lenses in our world, which caused him to see how limited his lenses were. . . . He said, 'I believe in a Supreme Being. I just don't think he entangles himself in all the religious stuff we get into'" (p. 20).

   Is Drew right? Is religion a good thing or a bad thing? If God were to create a religion, what would it look like? Be creative and have fun with this question!

3. "There is nothing less compelling than people who define themselves by what they are not" (p. 22).

   What are ways we define ourselves by what we are not? What are we really trying to communicate?

4. "Ryan met men and women from different cultures, became friends with those of different religions and spent time with

people of different sexual orientation. He discovered how tightly
he held to stereotypes and assumptions about people. In his
connection with others who were not like him, Ryan was continually challenged to confront his anxiety and fear. For the first
time he awoke to the depths of God's love and grace among men
and women considered by some to be beyond the loving reach
of God" (p. 24).

*Has there been a time when you've been surprised by the depth
of God's love and grace? What was that situation? How did your
understanding of God change because of it?*

5. "It's easy to spot people whose lives are open. They are neither
cynical about our world nor critical of others. In their depth and
maturity they are not easily offended. If anything, they seem
insatiably curious. When it comes to others and our world, their
first step is observation, not judgment. They are honest with
themselves, and when they speak, everyone seems to listen.
They are willing to be out front, to take risks and to be called
heretics because deep inside they know their way of seeing the
infinite, unchanging God is finite and changing" (pp. 25-26).

*In what ways and in what areas of your faith are you open?
Why? In what ways and in what areas of your faith are you
closed? Why?*

CHAPTER 2: FROM CERTAINTY TO PROBABILITY

1. "We often live with a desire to control things because it gives us
security and certainty. We want control so badly we even try to
control God. We like to think we can control how and where
and when he will act. It's almost as if we place boundaries
around him, box him in and create a framework for him. We
look for him in all the expected places, thinking he will work

within the small world we create for him. But God is not confined by our small plans, and he works in ways far outside our supposed span of control" (p. 29).

When is a time you have tried to control a situation or a person? What inside you was driving that? Was it security and certainty? Why are those things so important to us when it comes to faith?

2. "Last week a friend told me of a conversation he had with a person who said, 'I cannot understand how someone could be a Christian and a Republican.' Then, the very next day he had another conversation with someone who said, 'How can anyone be a Democrat and call themselves a Christian?' This really happened" (p. 31).

What causes many of us to divide so sharply along political lines, more often, it seems, than we do along religious lines?

3. "Those who assumed they were in and expected an invitation to the banquet were out. And those who believed there was no way they would ever receive an invitation to the banquet were in" (p. 32).

Read Jesus' parable about the banquet in Luke 14:15-23. How does this parable make you feel when you read it? Hopeful? Hopeless? Does it give you comfort or make you uncomfortable? What implications does this parable hold for us?

4. "No wonder the biblical writers describe God as light. He never changes but is faithful to respond to us and be exactly what we need him to be" (p. 36).

Share when you felt God respond to you in just the way you needed. How does he continually meet each of us where we are, yet remain the same?

5. "We all should ask Peter's question: Who are we to stand in

God's way? Who are we to draw lines, craft barriers, construct boxes, create in-groups and out-groups, and determine the ways and places God will work?" (p. 38).

We have to draw boundaries at some point, right? Or do we? Is that our job? Why or why not? And if we need to, then who gets to draw them?

CHAPTER 3: FROM DEFINITION TO DESCRIPTION

1. "Theology is an attempt to explain humanity's experience of the divine" (p. 42).

   What do you think of this definition of theology? Consider how this statement is fleshed out throughout the chapter. Discuss this among your group.

2. "Just as idols become gods, it's possible we can mistake our theology as the full explanation and complete understanding of God. Just as people bow to idols, we run the risk of bowing to our theology" (p. 44).

   How do we work against this to be sure we do not believe we have the "final word" about God? How do we remain humble yet confident in our changing faith?

3. "If you asked me to *define* my wife, I am not sure I could do it, because applying rigid, exacting words to her would defy who she is in every way. I say this because when we talk about people we love, defining them is not what we normally do, because relationships are dynamic and alive. They are always changing, growing and moving into new seasons" (p. 46).

   If this is what we do in our human relationships, then why do we operate so differently when it comes to our relationship with God? Why do we attempt to define him rather than describe him?

4. "Some may feel that our descriptions of God leave things wide open, and anyone can describe God however they see fit" (p. 48).

   Should this be of concern for us? Why?

5. "A theology that does not lead us to worship well could be bad theology" (p. 49).

   Share some examples when theology has seemed totally boring and stale. What would have to change to make theology become a worship experience?

CHAPTER 4: FROM WORDS TO EXPERIENCE

1. "Words carry meaning beyond their surface meaning. When spoken, certain phrases, words and names still give me a twinge of pain in my heart and soul. For most people they are mere words, but for me they stir up wounds and memories. These words are worse than sticks and stones that can bruise my bones" (p. 51).

   What are some words that stir emotions in you—both good and bad? If you are comfortable, take a moment to share some of those memories with one another. How should this lead us to be more mindful of how we use words?

2. "As powerful as they are, words also have limits. There are times when even the right words cannot communicate everything" (p. 54).

   How did you feel when you first read these words? When was a time you were left speechless or had a difficult time expressing the way you felt? Why does this happen?

3. "Millions of words will never do what one real experience can accomplish in us" (p. 56).

   Share an experience you have had that went far beyond words. Why does experience reach us in a way words cannot?

4. "God feels our pain so deeply that he cries out with us. His experience with us is so real words cannot capture it. It's God being there" (p. 57).

How does this statement strike you? What emotions does it evoke? Take a few minutes to share with your group. If you are comfortable, spend time praying for one another as you share.

CHAPTER 5: FROM KNOWING TO UNKNOWING

1. "We have more access to more information than ever before. While this does have an upside, we forget information is not always what we need. There are some things we can't find the answer to on Google. It may feel like we can know everything about anything, but it's not true" (p. 62).

Many believe more information is a good thing. What are times when it is not good? What, in your opinion, is more important than information?

2. "For a long time I did not think I should doubt, and I did all I could to keep it at bay. These days I am learning to no longer lock the door on it but welcome it in like an old friend. Doubt is not the enemy of faith but is essential to it" (p. 64).

How can doubt be essential to faith? Is it in any way dangerous to our faith? What has been your experience with doubt? Feel free to share with your group.

3. "They trust God enough to rage in front of him and ask probing questions. They knew there is no question we can bring to God that he cannot handle. The psalmists knew they did not know everything, and so they turned, in faith, to the one they believed did know everything and screamed their doubts at him" (p. 68).

Have you ever screamed at God in frustration? Have you ever accused God of not measuring up to or meeting your expectations? Are you comfortable with this idea? Why or why not?

4. "Both those who attempt to explain pain as part of God's good plan and those who argue against a good and powerful God do the same thing. They attempt to answer questions that defy any good explanation. Neither seems content to admit they do not or cannot know" (p. 70).

   Why do we so often strive for answers in the midst of difficult times?

5. "When Job came face to face with the Almighty, when his eyes had seen God he was overwhelmed by his unknowing. And in that place he rediscovered his faith. Job learned that what he did not know was the very thing that changed everything. As Richard Rohr points out, somehow 'unknowing becomes another kind of knowing'" (p. 72).

   What about Job's response seems to make sense? When we recognize that we will never fully comprehend God, it makes more things make sense. Why?

CHAPTER 6: FROM BEING RIGHT TO BEING FAITHFUL

1. "What are the right things to be wrong about?" (p. 76).

   Take some time to interact with this question, and observe why you and others respond the way you do.

2. "I know people who agree on the person of Jesus and could stand alongside one another and recite the Apostles' Creed with full conviction. Even still, there is one issue they cannot and will not agree on. Their disagreement is so big that in their minds they cannot worship together, because each side believes the other is wrong" (p. 76).

Why do many feel we have to believe exactly the same thing to be able to worship together? Do differing beliefs have to lead to division? Is it possible to believe different things about important issues and still be unified?

3. "Right now, as you read these words, there are things in our world we are unable to observe. There are questions we are unable to answer. If this is the case, how can we know with absolute certainty whether we are right or wrong? And will we be held accountable if we base our belief only on what we have the power to observe or understand? How can we judge something if we can't observe it or understand it correctly?" (p. 79).

Take some time and respond to these questions and their implications.

4. "A friend once said, 'That's just the way it is. There will be a lot of good people in hell.' So does that mean there will be a lot of bad people in heaven?" (pp. 81-82).

What does this say about our conceptions of right and wrong or good and bad? Will truly good people go to hell and some bad people go to heaven?

5. "We can have all the answers and not be right about anything" (p. 83).

We often seem convinced that being right is the most important thing. Why do we pursue being right, or at least not being wrong?

6. "Nowhere in the teachings of Jesus does he command his followers to be right, but he does call us to be faithful. Many refer to the Christian life as a 'relationship with Jesus.' What makes relationships work is not being right but living faithfully in them" (p. 83).

Think together about the time and energy many Christians have spent discussing (even arguing) about being right. What if that same energy was used to discuss how we can be faithful? How would our faith truly change if we sought to be faithful more than right?

CHAPTER 7: FROM POWER TO TRUTH

1. "We are willing to defend our truth because something in us seems to know truth and power are connected. When others believe we possess the truth, they see us as men and women of power, status and importance. This is why many arguments are not only about truth but also about power" (p. 90).

   Why do we so often desire power? What does power offer us that truth doesn't?

2. "Paul wanted that small church to be 'encouraged in heart and united in love.' He wanted them to know that all the power on display in the Roman Empire was not what's most important. Of real importance is being rooted in loving relationships with one another. Through this, they will come to know the truth of Christ Jesus. This is his ultimate hope for this church: to *know* Jesus, which is far different than *knowing about* Jesus" (p. 92).

   What's the difference between knowing *and* knowing about? *How does being "encouraged and united" move people toward knowing God?*

3. "Jesus did not fight, incite an uprising or stir up riots. Jesus, who claimed truth, was willing to give up power, even if it meant going to his death. In doing so, he showed what power really looks like" (p. 94).

   We often define power according to culture and history—its strength and might. But Jesus showed a different kind of power that was and still is considered weakness. Why are we so often unwilling to imitate this kind of power?

4. "Those who seemed to know a lot about God missed the truth of who Jesus was. But some knew exactly who he was, and they are the last people we think would know the truth: a demon-possessed man, a paralytic, a woman with vaginal bleeding, blind men, a pagan woman and the centurion at the foot of the cross" (p. 94).

The Gospels speak about God from the margins, from a place of weakness. How is this different from the world we live in today? Who are the people we often hear speak of God? Are they in a place of power and influence? If so, why do we look to them for an understanding of God?

5. "We must always remember the church is at its worst when it attempts to be the moral police of culture or the enforcer of truth. But we are at our best when we act as a healing agent in our world and extend to all people the loving hands of Jesus" (p. 99).

How would your faith change if you dedicated your life to living the truth of Jesus? What would others see? What arguments could they bring against you?

CHAPTER 8: FROM LEGALISM TO WHOLENESS

1. "We were routinely told our sin makes God angry—this kind of thinking is a gross reduction of the Christian faith" (p. 103).

Why has the story of an angry God been so popular for so long?

2. "If we are not careful, we may move from a culture that told us all the things we should *not* do to one that tells us all the things we *should* do. It's just more rules to be obeyed, and we may find people believing that if they are good at doing certain things, they are then good and godly. Being missional can become nothing more than a new form of legalism" (p. 104).

We seem beholden to rules, regulations and checklists. Why is this? What are the things in your life you believe you should do for God? Where does that belief come from?

3. "The transformed life is brand new territory. Jesus is more concerned with who people are, not what they do (or don't do). He knows that when people live out of a transformed heart, morals and mission will take care of themselves" (p. 105).

   How does it make you feel to know God cares more about who you are than what you can do or what you are able to not do?

4. "Without a transformed heart, our encounter with God would be too much for us, and any attempt to serve our world would fall flat" (p. 107).

   If a transformed heart is of utmost importance, then what does this suggest about how we think about a relationship with God? Do we place too much emphasis on other things? What needs to change about how we think of our faith?

5. "Jesus says to us, 'In the place of your worst failures, your biggest mistakes, your greatest shame, your dirtiest secret, your failing strength, your deepest wound, your messiest sin and devastating brokenness, I will plant my seeds of love, grace, compassion, hope, mercy, wholeness and healing. And in that place something new will grow that will put my splendor on display in you and through you so that the whole world will know that your stories don't have to end with ashes and mourning and despair. I am the One who rebuilds, renews and restores the places that have borne memories of grief and sorrow'" (pp. 110-11).

   What is your greatest mistake, your biggest regret? Do you see this as something that can and will be redeemed? Why or why not?

CHAPTER 9: FROM TOIL TO WORK

1. "I felt like my life didn't matter. What I mean is, if I had died back then I'm not real sure what people would have said at my funeral" (p. 116).

   Have you ever felt like this? Do you feel like this? What or who do you look to for meaning?

2. "When I talk about work, I'm talking about our calling or our *vocation*. The word *vocation* comes from the Latin word *vocare*, which means 'to call.' Frederick Buechner said vocation is 'the place where your deep gladness and the world's deep hunger meet'" (p. 119).

   Are you able to identify the place where your deep gladness meets the world's deep hunger? What is that place for you? Are you currently doing that? If not, what prevents you from doing that?

3. "Too often we have been led to believe that ministry is 'sacred work.' We speak of those who work in a local church as being in 'full-time ministry.' Many believe that working as a pastor or a missionary is more sacred than working as a waiter, a CEO, a bus driver or a salesperson. This belief is toxic" (p. 120).

   What has led us to believe that working in a church, as a missionary or for a nonprofit is somehow better work than others?

4. "All of us have an opportunity to work and experience a life that matters" (p. 121).

   In what ways can you, in your classroom, at your job or with your family, see the way God is working and join him in it? How would living out your calling change the way you view your job?

5. "If someone were to follow you around for a week, what would they say you are really about? What are the things you care about?

What do you spend most of your time paying attention to? How do you treat others? How do you view yourself?" (p. 125).

Take some time to contemplate and interact with these questions.

CHAPTER 10: FROM NOWHERE TO EVERYWHERE

1. "There was a time in my life when I tried to move past the idea of God, because I did not want to think about him or her—or whatever God might be. So I spent my time focused on others things and stopped paying attention to God" (p. 127).

   Have you ever felt like this? Perhaps you feel like this right now. Take a moment to share where you are or where you've been with regard to God.

2. "As much as the psalmists spoke of God being everywhere, they also had times when they shouted at God in complete exasperation. David wrote,

   > My God, my God, why have you forsaken me?
   >   Why are you so far from saving me,
   >   so far from my cries of anguish?
   > My God, I cry out by day, but you do not answer,
   >   by night, but I find no rest. (Psalm 22:1-2)

   These are the very words Jesus cried out as he hung on the cross. His experience was so dark in that moment; his own Father had abandoned him" (p. 129).

   How does it strike you to read how the psalmists spoke to God? It's almost as if they raised their fists and raged against him. Is this something you have been able to do? Is it something you would be comfortable doing? Why or why not?

3. "Sometimes God speaks through prayers and old hymns; other

times he speaks through Eminem. He is always present, always speaking everywhere; it's just a matter of whether we are willing to pay attention" (p. 134).

Do you agree with this idea? Why or why not? Are there ways and places God definitely does not speak?

4. "Many of us live very compartmentalized lives. Some places in our hearts are open, and we are okay talking about them. But then there are other places, spaces we don't like to go and certainly don't want God meddling in either. I know this all too well. I can compartmentalize parts of my life with the best of them" (p. 134).

Can you relate to this? Do you keep parts of your heart and life secret? Why? What would it be like to open up those parts of your heart?

5. "Perhaps our world is so broken precisely because too many of us have refused to interact with it. If things are really as dark as we think, why do many choose not to enter the darkness with the light?" (p. 137).

Why have so many Christians historically chosen to remove themselves from our dominant culture? What damage has this done? What would it look like to interact well with our world?

CHAPTER 11: FROM BAD NEWS TO GOOD NEWS

1. "While we believe the answer is Jesus, we're unaware of the questions people are asking. Chances are we give answers to questions no one is asking. And there is nothing more boring than an answer to a question that hasn't been asked" (p. 141).

What are some of the questions you hear people asking today? How have you responded well to those questions? What times have you not responded well?

2. "If those who wanted so badly to help me wouldn't take the time to listen, I wondered if they even cared about me at all. Looking back, I know I wasn't alone in feeling like this—not then and not now. When this happens, our normal response is to stop listening" (p. 143).

   When have you felt like someone was talking at you and not with you? How did you feel? Have you ever been guilty of speaking at someone—wanting to be heard more than wanting to listen?

3. "There is an ancient piece of wisdom that says, 'Give everybody the benefit of the doubt'" (p. 144).

   How would our day-to-day interactions with people—friends, classmates, children, coworkers, spouses—change if we constantly viewed them favorably? Discuss this together. Think about times when you have not given others the benefit of the doubt. Has there been a time when, after you've heard someone's story, your opinion of them and their behavior has changed?

4. "This is why the good news does not invite us to run from or fight against our pain. Nor should we pretend everything is okay. The good news is not a Band-Aid for an otherwise broken life. The good news is better than that" (p. 147).

   What would happen if instead of trying to explain away pain and brokenness, we spoke of the God who, in the person of Jesus, fully entered the human experience?

5. "He discovered their bad news and recognized it was the ragged opening for the good news" (p. 150).

   What keeps us from entering the pain of others to the point where we share in their pain? If this is what Jesus did, how might this change the way we think of inviting others into a changing faith?

CHAPTER 12: FROM FEAR TO LOVE

1. "My religious devotion was rooted in fear, which is why it took me a long time to believe in the God of love" (p. 153).

   How did you first experience God, and how has your faith changed since that time?

2. "In many ways, religion is an incubator for fear and shame. This is what I saw and experienced so many times" (p. 156).

   Take some time to interact with this statement. Have you ever experienced this? Why do you think we often use fear as a motivator? Is there any good that can come from this?

3. "The irony is we live such fearful lives while worshiping the very God who says to us over and over, 'Do not be afraid!' Perhaps if we reconsider who God is, we will see there is no reason to fear at all. We could stand with the psalmist and say, 'Whom then shall I fear?' We would hear his invitation to move from fear to love" (p. 158).

   What are some ways we can work against the kind of religion that stirs up fear? How can we cultivate God's love in the hearts of men and women in our world?

4. "What would it be like to live outside of fear, shame, anxiety, stress and worry? How would our lives look different if we were not ashamed of who we are in all our glory and brokenness? What if the good news for all people is that we have nothing to be afraid of? What would our world look like if we were not afraid of one another anymore? How would this kind of thinking lead us toward a changing faith?" (p. 159).

   There are several questions here. Take a moment and interact with each of them and take note of where your conversation goes.

CHAPTER 13: FROM SMALL STORIES TO A BIG STORY

1. "There are billions of people, families, beliefs, stories, experiences and cultures in our ever-changing world. And in the midst of it all there is one unchanging God knitting together a massive story, far bigger than any one place or time or person. He put all the divergent, seemingly disconnected parts together and invites us to experience being connected to something bigger. Because every story is bigger than any one person, it always involves other people, places and cultures" (p. 162).

   Does this statement seem overwhelming? At times it can feel like our story is lost in the midst of the bigger story at hand. Have you ever felt this way?

2. "And this is exactly what good stories do. They do not merely present information, they invite us to interact and participate with them. Our experiences provide points of connection; they open something inside us we might otherwise miss" (p. 165).

   Why do you love a good story? What experiences in your life have opened you to certain kinds of stories you now find irresistible?

3. "Humans have always told larger-than-life stories. We have developed stories, myths and legends that entire cultures identify with. These stories connect us. They are the glue that holds us together and give us a framework for understanding and meaning" (p. 166).

   What are the stories we believe and embrace as a culture? What stories unites our friends, families and faith? What causes these stories to endure?

4. "Our stories are an important part of the larger whole, and what we choose to do matters both now and forever. This is how God

is telling his story, through everyday people like you and me. No matter how much our world changes or we change, the big story does not. There is great freedom in that" (p. 167).

How have you seen God telling his story in your life?

5. "While yesterday, today and tomorrow may change, we serve a God who does not. Even though our world and our stories change, there is an unchanging God telling a cosmic story of redemption, renewal and restoration that does not change, and he invites us into a changing faith" (p. 168).

   Return to the list of questions and doubts about God, life, faith, spirituality and religion you wrote down at the beginning of this book. How do you feel about some of those questions now? Better? Worse? The same? Engage those questions again with your group and discuss how you feel about them now.

Also available from Michael Hidalgo

BEING FOUND BY THE **ONE** WE ARE LOOKING FOR

UNlost

MICHAEL HIDALGO

Praise for *Unlost:*

"In this wonderful book Michael Hidalgo reminds us that the gospel is good news! Through . . . winsome narrative, *Unlost* rehearses how our personal stories connect with God's story. Without sugarcoating our challenges, the book inspires hope and confidence in the relationship that God desires with us. This is a great book for anyone who wants to explore their connection with God or who needs to be reenergized spiritually."

Reggie McNeal, author of *Get Off Your Donkey! Help Somebody and Help Yourself*

"*Unlost* reminds us that when God pursues us, fear does not have the last word."

Rebekah Lyons, author of *Freefall to Fly*